THE OPEN HEART

by

ROSALIND RINKER

OF THE ZONDERVAN CORPORATION
GRAND RAPIDS, MICHIGAN 49506

To my little sister

MARGARET RINKER HALLADAY

Second printing, slightly revised March 1970
Third printing September 1970
Fourth printing December 1970
Fifth printing May 1972
Sixth printing November 1972
Seventh printing January 1974
Eighth printing September 1974

Library of Congress Catalog Card Number 76-81065

Scripture versions used in this book:

All undesignated Scripture is King James Version (KJV).
The following versions or translations have been used by permission:

The Amplified New Testament © copyright 1958 by Lockman Foundation (Grand Rapids: Zondervan Publishing House).

The Berkeley Version in Modern English © copyright 1959 by Zondervan Publishing House (Grand Rapids: Zondervan Publishing House).

Printed in the United States of America

Contents

Preface

Books are like children. They are part of you. Once they're here, you accept them as they are, for they are just what they are . . . and more.

Books like children are often closed until some discerning person takes time to open them up and discover their real potential.

This book first came out in 1963, titled, *On Being A Christian.* Later it was changed to *Becoming a Christian.* At the time, I thought the message of this book was a sequel to *You can Witness With Confidence,* for it illustrated the varying ways by which God reaches out in love to claim His own.

Then one day the true message of this book was revealed to me by a little lady asking for an autograph. She stood there, apologizing for her dog-eared copy. "I am a missionary's wife," she explained. "They sent me home from the field because I was on the verge of a nervous breakdown. I couldn't even read my Bible. But this book (a gift to me) prevented me from going over the edge. In it I found the tender, patient, never changing love of God on every page. My sanity was restored. Look — I've underlined every place where you mention God's Love."

I was impressed as I leafed through the book at the red markings on every page. "I'll have to read this book again," I promised myself. I did, and this revised volume is the result.

The Open Heart speaks on a personal level. It reveals a clear step-by-step portrayal of what the Christian experience is all about.

ROSALIND RINKER

Chicago 1969

THE JOURNEY AHEAD

WHEN ONE IS GOING SOMEWHERE, the first step is preparation. We are going on a journey together, a most important and interesting journey. The destination lies through a certain Door, and there is great treasure awaiting you. The destination is the Kingdom of God. Progressively, we must all become Knockers, Askers, Seekers.

The directions are clear and loud:

> *The one who asks will always receive; the one who is searching will always find, and the door is opened to the man who knocks* (Matthew 7:8, *Phillips*).

The preparation begins in your attitude, or to be more specific, in your heart. You must become as a little child in all openness and willingness. This is your part. The rest will be prepared for you.

Faith is putting your hand into the hand of Jesus Christ. Even in the darkness of unbelief, He will hold fast, because He is Light. He knows the way.

"Lord, I believe; help thou mine unbelief," is an authentic prayer (Mark 9:24).

Asking is not difficult, except when one is uncertain what to ask for. Ask for a child-like spirit. Ask for an open, willing heart. Ask for the heart you need. If your asking fails to materialize, try again. You will learn in the process. The goal is to meet your God personally, for the first time or in a deeper way. He'll be with you all the time, but you may not always recognize Him.

When this new life comes to you, and the certainty that you are loved, forgiven and accepted breaks over you, the whole world becomes new. What has happened to you is so joyful and exciting that it is quite natural for you to feel like a new person.

The Apostle Paul has this to say about what happened to him:

> *For if a man is in Christ he becomes a new person altogether — the past is finished and gone, everything has become fresh and new* (II Corinthians 5:17, *Phillips*).

God loves you. His love surrounds you with gifts constantly and unconditionally — in the natural world. However, when spiritual springtime comes, your heart will awaken and the living seed planted within will respond.

A Christian is onc who is responding to Jesus Christ. He said:

> *I myself am the road (the way, . . . unto the Father. . . .* KJV*). The man who has seen me has seen the Father. . . . The man who comes to me will never be hungry and the man who believes in me will never again be thirsty* (John 14:6, 8, 9; 6:35, *Phillips*).

> *Nobody comes to me unless he is drawn to me by the Father who sent me, and I will raise him up when the last day comes* (John 6:44, *Phillips*).

ROSALIND RINKER

Part I

MEET THE PEOPLE GOD LOVES

Who Is a Christian?

From the teachings of Jesus Christ

1. One who hears Christ's voice, because he is one of his sheep. John 10:3, 16, 27.
2. One to whom Christ has been revealed. Luke 10: 22.
3. One whom the Father draws to Jesus. John 6:44.
4. One who comes to Jesus and learns of Him. Matthew 11:28, 29.
5. One who sees and believes in Jesus. John 6:40.
6. One who hears Christ's voice and opens the door. Revelation 3:20.
7. One whom the Father gives to Jesus. John 6:37.
8. One who goes through the Door. John 10:9.
9. One who eats of the living Bread. John 6:35, 58.
10. One who thirsts, comes, and drinks. John 7:37.
11. One who is born anew of the Spirit. John 3:5, 6.
12. One who loves his brother. John 13:34, 35.
13. One who loves his enemy. Matthew 5:44, 45.
14. One who loves the Lord God. Mark 12:29, 30.
15. One who loves his neighbor as himself. Mark 12: 31.

Suggested use: Prepare slips of paper with one reference on each and pass them out previously, asking each person to give a 3-minute talk on his reference. Leave time for discussion, questions and prayer.

Creative suggestions will be given to you for your own group, for all the following lessons, as you pray and meditate. Whatever makes for simple, practical and personal application should be your guide.

1

The Searching Heart: a traveler

As an introduction to the coming chapters, this is a retelling of familiar truths in an allegorical style.

"ONLY ONE DOOR?" questioned the Searching-Heart, an earth-dweller who is inquiring the way to Eternal Existence. "Every house has a back door as well as a front door. Why only *one* door?"

"Yes, only one Door, but many roads lead to the Door," cautioned the Wise-one.

"Many roads? How shall I know I'm on the right one?"

"There is no way for *me* to know which of the many roads is to be your road," said the Wise-one. "Each earth-dweller has his own road, and if he listens, he'll find his road leading into The Way."

"Listens? Listens to whom? Whom shall I ask?"

"You may listen to other travelers," said the Wise-one, "and there are thousands. Many will wish to talk for hours with you. Others . . . you must *ask* to get information. Only . . . let me warn you. There are two kinds of travelers. First, those who have found the Door, and are at liberty to go in and out on business for their Kind. Second, those who are searching for The Way to the Door."

"Oh, thank you, thank you," said Searching-Heart. "That should make it quite simple. I'll just be sure to ask someone who has already found the Door. He'll be able to tell me."

"Well, now — that's exactly what I warned you about a moment ago," cautioned the Wise-one. "Already you have forgotten what I said. Listen carefully."

"There are many roads to the Door. Each traveler is going somewhere. Some know where they want to go, and others don't know—they just follow along. The earth is full of all kinds of roads with broad avenues leading to all sorts of gods and religions, self-development cults, pleasures and diversions. Some of these roads lead to Nowhere and to Unmentionable Destinations from which no one has ever returned." With this, he fell silent, stirring the dust at his feet with the little stick he held in his hand.

Searching-Heart was impatient. "Old Wise-one, you didn't hear me. I *said* I would ask directions of those who have *already* found the Door, not those who've never been there!"

"Yes, yes," said the Old-one slowly. "I heard you. Why don't you sit down here beside me in the shade? We'll talk about these things. There is no hurry. Nobody ever got anywhere in a hurry. Everything God makes grows slowly, takes root, and brings forth. Sit down."

"I suppose he's right," said Searching-Heart to himself, as he sat down on a convenient rock. "When I think of how little things in my life have turned into God's directive care and love, I know He's put them there."

"You know," he continued, "I haven't always been known as Searching-Heart. I had goals of my own to achieve but I became very tired and bored. Nothing I ever mastered satisfied me. I finally decided to go on a personal search. Then someone told me that if I ever got to *the Door* and knocked, my search would be over. Help me, Wise-one. I shall be ever so grateful."

"Ah, yes, you are a Searching-Heart. I knew that by the tone of your voice and the look in your eye even before you told me," chuckled the Old-one. "I'm not easily fooled any more; but I can't go with you. You'll have to learn for yourself about asking and receiving directions."

"The travelers, Old-one, you were going to tell me about, which travelers could give me the *right* directions," reminded Searching-Heart.

"Yes, the travelers. Now, about asking directions, there are two troublesome things I want to tell you, and you must keep them firmly in mind or you'll be wasting your time. One is, that you can't tell them by their dress nor even by their speech. (Some of them think this is quite important!) Second, each man will tell you of *his own* road to the Door, and how he found The Way. You'll have to be careful, for this may or may not be the right road for *you*."

"Tell me more. I want to hear more. Tell me about their appearance first. How will I know them?"

"Their appearance? Some appear to have found the Door and give that impression when they've never been in sight of the Door! Their undiscovered motives may be all right, but they are still ignorant, and the Truth about the King and the kingdom is not in their hearts. They are all wrapped up in their own interpretations and cogitations."

"And those who have found?" prompted the Searcher.

"Those who have entered the Door, and are out on the King's business, appear to be all things to all men in order that they may reach through the superficialities of human thought, and work together with the King in directing those who are ready to respond."

"Ah," said the Searcher with eagerness. "Then it will be of these travelers I will ask my questions. But — *how* did you say I would know them? Tell me again."

"You will know them," explained the Wise-one, "by the light in their eye (which will illumine their body) and by the love they have for each other. When you find one like this, cleave unto him, learn from him all your heart desires. Only — I warn you about that second troublesome thing." He paused to let the Searcher name it.

"You mean, how to find The Way to the Door?"

"Yes, and no. I mean the explanations each Light-traveler will give you will be that which led *him* to The Way. Remember, I told you, each traveler journeys on his own road, this is his own life, his Life-road. The circumstances which brought him to The Way and finally to the Door, may or may not be the right ones for you. The King has a way of knowing about *you* and what Life-road you should take. These travelers-with-a-light-in-their eye will direct you to The Way, but listen carefully. Do not always act immediately. Listen and wait."

"Wait for what? Listen for what?"

"For the Voice of the Silent Messenger. Then you'll be certain. You must be sure." The Old-one nodded his head for emphasis. "You must be sure."

"The Silent Messenger? Tell me who He is?"

"The King has a Silent Messenger who communicates with all open hearts, with all listening hearts. He is speaking all the time, all the time, all the time." He paused a moment to let this sink in. Then he continued, "This Messenger is invisible and silent, but — it is an audible silence; that is, He speaks within your heart. You'll know when He speaks. Your heart will know. You've probably already heard His voice and haven't recognized Him. You'll find yourself going in the right direction. He'll confirm it and lead you right to the Door."

"Old-one, you speak in riddles! About spirits and ghosts! Give me something more definite! I want to know everything. I want to find The Way to the Door. I mean to enter that Door and become a part of that Kingdom."

"You are already blessed!" The Wise-one lifted his hands in wonder and in benediction. "The Messenger has already communicated with you. Your willpower has already been motivated. You were an *Asker* — now you are a *Seeker*. Your name is now Seeker-of-the-Door. Soon. Very soon. You are among the blessed! Have courage!"

The Searcher had one more question. "Wise-one, when you speak of The Way to the Door, is this the name of a road I should look for?"

"No, it is the name of a Person: the Person who is also the Door. This Person is The Good Shepherd — The Way, The Truth and The Life. Your encounter with Him will be alone no matter who else may be present. Your knock will in reality be only a *response* to the strong urge you are now feeling, the drawing as of a magnet which is within you. When you knock at the Door it will be opened. All freedom, joy, light, and love are within, for they are rivers which flow from His Person.

"Your searching heart will know the Shepherd's Voice. Your search will be ended when you meet Him face to face."

For Discussion

1. Why has the author used an allegorical style for this chapter? Can you name other authors who have thus helped us to re-think our beliefs?
2. As home work: Ask each to read this chapter, and find Scriptures which have (or can) contribute to ideas presented. Discuss these in class.
3. Class work: Read the chapter aloud, using three persons: the narrator, and the two characters.
4. Let the rest of the group give their personal reactions to specific areas thus presented.

2

The Open Heart: a three-year-old

Behold I stand at the door and knock. If anyone listens to My voice and opens the door, I will come in to him and dine with him and he with Me (Revelation 3:20, *Berkeley*).

SETTING OF THE STORY: It is Christmas, and the holiday atmosphere fills the Rice home. Kathleen, a blonde, curly-haired little girl of three years is seated on her mother's lap with a book in her hands, looking at a picture of the wise men on camels.

Kathleen: Mother, where are the wise men going?

Mother: They are going to see Jesus, darling.

Kathleen: Where does Jesus live?

Mother: Up in heaven. (Then, thinking she had better be more specific) Jesus lives in our hearts if we ask Him to.

Kathleen: (With her eyes shut) Lord Jesus, come live in my heart. (Then opening her eyes and looking around) But Mother, I can't see Jesus.

Mother: No, Kathleen, but if you stay real quiet and listen you can hear Jesus' voice down inside your heart.

Kathleen: (Sits for a moment with her eyes shut tightly, then opens her big blue eyes with excitement) Yes, I can hear Jesus' voice down inside my heart.

Mother: What does He say?

Kathleen: Jesus says, Don't cry Kathleen, don't stamp your feet and don't say darn-it! (Then addressing Jesus once more with her eyes shut) And Jesus, you be a good Boy and don't ever come out of my heart!

(The same living room five years later; father and daughter are present)

Kathleen: (Now eight years old) Daddy, tell me, am I really a Christian?

Father: Yes, dear, you are. Why do you ask?

Kathleen: The other kids at school say I'm *not*, because I don't remember *when* I became a Christian!

Father: Perhaps you were too young to remember. You were only three years old (and he repeated the story that took place during that Christmas season). After you asked Jesus to come into your heart, He did.

Kathleen: Yes, He did, and He never left, did He! Oh, I wish you had told me before!

Father: Well, now you know. Let's kneel together and you tell the Lord Jesus again, so you'll *know* when you said it, and you'll never have to wonder again if you're really a Christian.

The heart of a child is an open heart with eyes to see the invisible and ears to hear the still small Voice. The heart of a child is an open, responsive heart. Because of the pictures of Jesus Christ and the stories about Him, He is real to them. Instinctively, out of this background, their prayers are addressed, Dear Jesus, instead of Dear Heavenly Father. Their prayers are direct, honest, personal, and often humorous.

Kathleen had a wise mother who herself was responsive to the Spirit when it came to taking advantage of the present opportunity, and making spiritual truth live for her child. The child needed no urging, no pressure, no explanation of doctrine. Her little, open heart walked right into the deep truth over which wise men stumble.

Kathleen also had a wise father who did not try to make her believe something she couldn't remember. She didn't need to remember. She just needed to know that the Lord Jesus is always present, always with her, always available. Christ has already done His part in coming to this earth, in His life, His death and His resurrection. Her part was to respond to Him, and she did.

Was Kathleen's conversion a valid one? Some parents do not think their children should be encouraged to make a decision so young in life; they feel the very young are too easily subject to undue influence. However, in the case of Kathleen, you will notice that it was merely the power of suggestion inherent in her mother's statement, "Jesus lives in our hearts if we ask Him to," that prompted Kathleen of her own little will to invite Jesus into her heart.

Have you ever noticed that most children seem to be born with truth and faith? Not until they are hurt and disillusioned by their elders do they begin to register doubts and unbeliefs. I'm not saying that children are born with *all* good traits, because selfish possession is also inherent in them! However, it seems that the older we become, the more we need urging and prodding by our teachers to act on spiritual truth.

Yes, Kathleen's conversion was a valid one. I've known the family for years. Mildred Rice is one of my best friends. Kathleen is a lovely, mature young lady, a college graduate, and now counseling others. She has a deep, loving concern for others, teaching them to know Jesus Christ, and is active in church and various groups.

There is another observation I'd like to make. In the twelve years I was active as a counselor of college students, it was very apparent that the young people who had childhood training in Jesus Christ were more sensitive to any approach regarding Him. Those who could recall a prayer time, a decision time, or something similar, were more responsive than those who had no such experience. The living Word of God, once planted in the heart, takes root quietly. If not nourished, it remains dormant until the love of God reaching through circumstances and response, bring a Spiritual Springtime (a new birth) into the heart.

Parents who are so broad-minded that they do not wish their children to have any religious influence until they are old enough to know what they are doing, deprive their children of a great spiritual heritage. The unseen, imaginative, or spiritual worlds are more real to a child than the material world in which he lives. The very root of all creative activity lies in the imagination, and if that is blunted, unwatered, or forced back during childhood, how handicapped a child can be! On the other hand, there are parents who send their children to Sunday school when they themselves never darken the door of a church. They want their children to have definite rootlets of faith in God and trust in Jesus Christ.

There is a better way: You parents may lead your own children to Christ, who is the Door. One mother used the suggested picture in Revelation 3:20 with her daughter. "Jesus is standing at the door, the heart's door, and knocking. He wants to come in and live there." She asked her daughter to read the verse for herself and find what *her part* was, what she should do. And she did it. Her open heart responded to Christ and received Him.

Another mother shared her concern over her fourteen-year-old-son. "I don't even know if he's given his heart to Christ," she told me.

"Why don't you ask him?" I suggested.

The next morning her face told me the story before her words! The night before, she waited for her son's return, and after he closed the front door behind him, she said, "Charles, I want to ask you a question — I've been thinking a great deal about it and I think the only way I'll find out is to ask you."

"What is it, Mother?"

"Have you ever given your heart to Jesus Christ?"

"No, I never have, but I'd like to."

"How about doing it right now — with me?" Mother and son knelt and prayed together for the first time in their lives.

There is no mountain of difficulty too great for you to remove if you ask and believe, said Jesus. That mother believed, asked and acted on the faith God gave her, and it came to pass. You will know when to ask the question, how to ask it, what to say to your child. And your child will always be able to say, "My mother (or father) led me to Jesus Christ."

> *I tell you, therefore: Whatever you ask in prayer, believe that you received it and it shall be yours* (Mark 11:24, *Berkeley*).

Jesus through a little child, illustrated what He meant when He answered the question, "Who is the greatest in the kingdom of heaven?"

"Believe me," he said, "unless you change your whole outlook (be converted, KJV) and become like little children you will never enter the kingdom of Heaven. It is the man who can be as humble as this little child who is greatest in the kingdom of Heaven" (Matthew 18:3, 4, *Phillips*).

Someone has pointed out that there are three steps:

1. "change your whole outlook — be converted" — a new direction;
2. "become like little children" — a new spirit;
3. "enter the kingdom of Heaven" — a new sphere of living.

Obviously, no man can do these things by mere wishing, nor even by self-directed willpower. But the moment your wish becomes a prayer, and your will is directed to Christ, He is there. He's always been there waiting for this moment in your life. If your heart is un-childlike — ask! If your heart seems closed — ask! If your heart needs opening — ask! Christ's coming into your heart means you are given a new spirit, the spirit of a little child. You will have a fresh beginning and enter a new sphere of living, with His power and His presence to face life and to love others.

In the imaginative part of your mind's eye, see your heart opening like a flower in response to the warmth and love of the Son of God who loved you and died for you — to become His child, and give thanks.

For Discussion

1. Read aloud: Matthew 18:1-4. Luke 10:21-22.
2. Discuss the validity, and the importance of a childhood decision, or response, to Christ.
3. Base that discussion on the illustrations in this chapter, and the experiences of group members.

Prayer Time

Silently Meditate on the last paragraph in this chapter and visualize (with eyes closed for concentration):

1. Your own heart opening up.
2. The heart of your child (children).
3. The heart of some other child, whose name may come to your attention while you are praying.

Audibly Claim the promise of Mark 11:22-25

1. Pray by name for children known to you.
2. Pray for an opportunity to speak to him, with simplicity and love. Ask *the* question. Expect an affirmative answer.
3. Pray for courage to offer a short prayer of thanks with that child, for a "sealing" memory.

3

The Willing Heart: my own experience

> *As for you, my son . . . acknowledge your father's God, and serve Him wholeheartedly with a willing mind, for the Lord searches all hearts and understands every development of the thoughts . . .* (I Chronicles 28:9, *Berkeley*).

MY OWN CONVERSION EXPERIENCE was a simple one and a willing one. I can never remember any time in my life when I was not consciously aware of God.

As a child, I attended a little Methodist church in New Rockford, North Dakota. My father went there as a young lawyer when the state was still a territory; my mother had just finished her degree at the University of Minnesota and accepted a position as principal of the city school.

Since father was Sunday school superintendent, all six of us attended church and Sunday school without question. I've always believed in God and Jesus Christ and the Bible — everyone did, I thought. It was not until I was a sophomore in high school that my mother became concerned about me; mainly I think because I made the girls' basketball team, and traveled to other towns on weekends with both teams.

Sixty miles south of us, outside the city of Jamestown, in a beautiful grove by the River James (Jim River to us kids who swam in it), an old-fashioned camp meeting was held yearly. Mother drove down, taking my high school friend, Harriet, and me. There at the young people's conference, for the first time in my life, I heard people give personal testimony about what it meant to have Jesus Christ in their hearts. There was a tone in their voices, a look on their faces when they talked about Him, that I'd never experienced before. I wanted what they had.

Then someone asked me a face-to-face question. "Have you ever given your heart to Jesus Christ? Have you accepted Him as your Saviour?" That was all I needed. That question was my invitation. I knew I had never done this consciously and definitely. I "believed" in Him, but — no, I had never given myself to Him.

"No, I never have."

"Would you like to?" was the next question.

My reply was instant. "Yes, I would." However, when I was urged to go forward to the altar to pray, I resisted. It was my first day; I wanted to see what happened to the others.

By evening of that same day, I was ready to "go forward," but I felt that I had to wait for the "altar call"! I didn't know then that my decision had already been made, that the drawing power of God's love was already drawing me to Christ. I sat on the end seat in about the fourth row. I knew what I was going to do and I did it. I knelt a moment at the altar, then almost at once got to my feet, for in that split second something happened. Someone met me! I had knocked and the Door had opened! The heaviness disappeared, a great light shone in and around me — or so it seemed to me. I had given myself to Jesus Christ without even saying the words — from my very heart, and He had received me. My mother was right there behind me; I threw my arms around her and cried for joy.

They called it "being converted," or "being born again." A new dimension was added to my life; from that moment I belonged to Jesus Christ. I wanted to do His will and be the kind of person He wanted me to be. I remember two nights later making that trip to the altar again, this time answering another invitation: to give myself for "full-time Christian service" as a missionary, or wherever God might direct me.

I had a willing heart that responded to the first personal invitation I ever received. Perhaps it is because of this and the way it changed the course of my life, that I'm particularly interested in teenagers. Every time I have an opportunity I find myself asking some young man or woman this question: "Have you ever given your heart to Jesus Christ? Have you accepted Him as your Saviour?"

I believe there are willing hearts everywhere, ready to believe and ready to respond.

> *Every one who has listened to and has learned of My Father comes to Me* (John 6:45, *Berkeley*).

For Discussion

1. Discuss the three verbs in the Scripture at the close of this chapter.
2. Let each share personally how, or when, or to what extent he has personally responded to Christ.

Prayer Time

1. Seven out of twelve men in an Indianapolis study group agreed to put their *response to Christ* into words for the first time (audibly) in their lives, after reading this chapter.
2. What would your group like to do?

4

The Thankful Heart: Episcopal women and military wives

> *It was nothing you could or did achieve — it was God's gift of grace which saved you. No one can pride himself upon earning the love of God. The fact is that what we are we owe to the hand of God upon us. For we are his workmanship, created in Christ Jesus to do those good deeds which God planned for us to do* (Ephesians 2:8-10, *Phillips*).

IN THIS CHAPTER I'd like to share an exciting discovery revealed to me during the last several years. It isn't a new truth, but its meaning has become new to me.

It is this: Gratitude can be a road leading to the Door of Eternal Life. Recognizing any part of the Gift or the Giver is one of the first steps to the Door. The new life in Christ is a gift to be received. It does not need to be earned, nor worked for, and it cannot be bought or sold.

One day it became real for the Apostle Paul, too. The words at the beginning of this chapter are one of the ways he has expressed it.

We've discovered four characteristics that can be common to all who want to become a Christian — the heart that is searching, open, willing and responsive. Some persons find the Saviour they are looking for; others are found by the Good Shepherd when they didn't even know they were lost. The children didn't know they were lost; at fifteen years of age, I didn't realize I needed a Saviour. Jesus Christ knew we needed Him and brought us to Himself. This is the kind of love God has for earth-people; He has already prepared forgiveness, welcome, and a joyous homecoming for us.

A person may be the possessor of any combination of heart-attitudes. The Thankful Heart to be described in this chapter is also a responsive, open, willing heart, but that doesn't mean it always has been.

Before one can be thankful, there is a condition to be fulfilled. A gift must be given and received, then one can be thankful. The giving of thanks is the completion of a lovely transaction. Someone had a loving thought. Someone planned, prepared and made ready. It is only the immature or the selfish who receive without giving thanks.

This whole world in which we live is a gift from God. The very body we live in is a gift from Him; He intended it should bring us joy and fulfillment. He prepared the fresh air for us; He prepared colors for our eyes, movement for our bodies; living, growing things of earth to delight and entertain us. He even gave us to each other for the fulfillment of our emotional, social, and intellectual needs. And He has given Himself to us as the fulfillment of our spiritual needs.

As a growing child, I must have been obnoxious. I had to learn to receive gifts and to be thankful. I remember that process, and of learning that someone went to the trouble of selecting something for me. I remember that gifts at Christmas or birthdays usually fell short of my expectations. Now I know that this is plain selfishness. I was thinking of what I wanted, what I didn't get, and what I'd do with what had been given me when I couldn't use it and didn't want it. I had to learn to give thanks and to think of the one who prepared a gift for me. Then I began to take joy in giving, in preparing for others, in planning to give a gift.

Isn't it the same thing when it comes to being a

Christian? My experience of becoming a Christian was a gift to me and I was grateful to a point. The point was, I wanted others to enjoy the same religious experience I'd had. For years my emphasis was right there — on the experience, how to get converted, how to become wholly committed to God, how to get old sins out of the way. Then I discovered the Giver! I discovered who Jesus Christ really was, that He and the Father are One, that He is the mighty Creator, the Giver of all good and perfect gifts (Colossians 1:16-19).

In all my books I speak of this discovery, for it transformed everything for me. My Bible became a new book, my outlook was new, my emphasis in teaching became Christ-centered instead of experience-centered. The whole world became a gift of God. My book, *Prayer—Conversing With God*, grew out of the necessity of bringing people face-to-face with Christ, speaking to Him from their open hearts, and starting with thanksgiving.

Then to my utter astonishment, my tree of faith broke out of its "greenhouse" again! The little mustard seed of faith which was planted in my heart when I became a Christian, grew and kept on growing, as the Lord Jesus said it would (Matthew 13:31, 32).

Many times I've tried to confine this new life by doctrinal or experimental boundaries, until I felt I had things pretty well defined. And then — God would do some new thing in someone's heart that would utterly astonish me! And I would have to confess that He and His ways are greater, infinitely greater, than my ways of trying to define and confine Him!

What I mean is this. After I'd worked things out so I could share my experience of conversion, and teach the meaning of repentance, confession, faith and salvation from the Bible so that others could come into this experience, too, I found that people were converted by ways I had never thought of. That the center touchstone of faith is Jesus Christ Himself! Knowledge of the above mentioned truths are good, but they can come either before or after the conversion experience.

The experience, or the giving of the gift of salvation, was paramount to me in importance until I discovered that the Giver was more important; because in truth, the Giver becomes the Gift! And since then, I've noticed that people who continue to emphasize the Gift, without much mention of the Giver, become rigid and exacting when others do not use all the "salvation terms" they think are necessary. Since knowing the nature of the Giver, I know He will carry out His purpose and finish what He begins. He is great enough. I can trust Him with His own.

Yes, God broke out of the little box in which I had placed Him. When I began to teach people who had never prayed aloud, to pray directly from their hearts and forget the Shakespearean prayer-language, they were converted! People who'd never prayed before, found the Door opened when they prayed to Jesus Christ from their open hearts.

What amazed me was the prayer I taught them was one of thankfulness, not of repentance. Not that I intended to substitute one for the other, but as the first step on the stairway to the Door, God seemed to be leading me to teach gratitude. Then, praying a simple prayer of thankfulness, people began to meet Jesus Christ! The Door was wide open, and the light of God poured into their hearts. And all this without audibly confessing that they were sinners, and going through the "outline" I'd previously been using! Incredible and impossible! Amazing! And yet true!

Before I go further, telling you about my discoveries regarding thankful hearts and what God taught me through them, I want to tell you several true stories. I was there as an eye-witness. Please bear in mind that teaching was being given on the very personal quality of God's love: *God loves you.* Also, on the fact that

Christ is present, here and now, and His love is unconditional (Matthew 18:19, 20).

Episcopal Women

The scene about to be described was the first of five sessions in a School of Prayer in an Episcopal church. Our first lesson was from Matthew 18:19, 20: "Jesus Christ is here with us, present with us; He loves us eternally. And we? We have gone our own ways and never lifted our voices audibly without the aid of the Prayer Book to thank Him either for the Gifts given, or that He is the Giver."

There were twelve women present. Not one of them had ever prayed aloud in front of another. They were in fact both afraid of their own voices and ashamed to fail, but they wanted to "break the sound barrier" and speak to Christ face-to-face. We were standing together in a little circle, with arms linked (for moral support).

Counselor: *Jesus is here!* The marvel of His love and care never really dawns on us until we voice our thanks to Him. He wants to hear you speak to Him. (Pause) For *what* are you the most grateful? Or for *whom* are you most grateful? A simple sentence, or part sentence will do. *Thank You, Lord,* for . . . you finish it. Say it in your heart first, then aloud. You'll know when it's your turn, because your heart will pound! That's God, pouring more adrenalin into your system to help you get started! (A quiet pause of a moment).

Dorothy B: Thank You, Lord, for this church.

Elly E: Thank You, Lord, for my husband and son.

Counselor: Thank You, Lord, that You are here.

Esther B: Thank You, Lord, for my family.

Mary D: And thank You, Lord, for mine.

Mary Ann C: Thank You, Lord, for this new little life within me.

Mim B: Thank You, Lord, that You love me.

Alice H: And thank You, Lord, for making me *want*

to pray. (Each one present prayed a thankful prayer and the counselor closed the prayer time.) Next day. Before class session, Mary Ann rushed into the room.

Mary Ann: What *happened* to me yesterday? What happened?

Counselor: Well, *you* tell me what happened to you.

Mary Ann: You know, it was the first time I ever prayed aloud, breaking that "sound barrier," you called it. Do you remember what I prayed? (Looking up with a twinkle in her eye. She was five or six months pregnant.)

Counselor: Yes, I remember very well.

Mary Ann: I meant it. I meant it when I prayed that *Thank You, Lord, for this new little life within me.* I meant it with all my heart. It was the first time I ever spoke to Jesus knowing who He really was. When I got into my car after class, I found myself saying, Thank You, Lord, for this car. Thank You, Lord, for my husband. When I got home: Thank You, Lord, for this lovely home. Thank You, Lord, for everything! The refrigerator, the rugs, the silver, the furniture! (She stopped for breath.) I was *full* of thanksgiving and I was *full* of light, and I want to sing and sing! (Stopping for a second) Tell me, what *happened* to me?

Counselor: You've just told me. You let the Lord Jesus come into your heart. Your being thankful opened the Door, because you knew to Whom you were talking. You acknowledged by that heart-prayer that He is the Giver of all life. You let Him come in.

Mary Ann: Yes, yes, that's it. Christ is in me. I know it, I feel it! Then — is this — is this being converted?

Counselor: Yes, it certainly is!

Unconventional as it seemed to me, who am I to question God's ways of birth? Up until this time, Mary Ann had had a strong church background, but with an impersonal faith. It was the Road of Thankfulness that opened this pilgrim's heart, and she found herself through the Door, singing and winging! (P.S. After the series was finished, Mary Ann started a little class among her own friends, with more miracles of faith taking place.)

This was the first one. After that, I witnessed many others coming into newness of life as they gave thanks to the Lord Jesus for simple things.

Military Wives

I must tell you about two women whose husbands are both officers in the USAF. I had been invited to speak at a weekend conference. Joan F. was an extroverted, jolly person who was the mother of five children. When she got into the backseat of the car, driving to the conference, she remarked: "Well, I hear you've written some books. What've you written about?"

"The one people seem to like the most is about prayer." Then wanting to make a quick bridge across to her: "I'm interested in helping people to pray from their hearts, short and sweet — instead of beating around the bush with lengthy prayers."

"We-ll," she sort of drawled out, "Sounds like that's for me."

I watched her during the first two meetings while I was teaching on the nature of God, His great personal love and care and presence, His knowing, and His power. At the close of each meeting, four groups formed to discuss things at closer range. After the second time, she came over to me and I knew before she spoke what was on her mind.

"What about me, Ros? What does a New Englander like me, who is a cold Congregationalist to boot, what does she do?"

Looking into her eyes, I knew God loved her and had brought her to this moment. Instantly it was given to me what to do next. "Whom do you know here, pretty well?" I questioned. Joan motioned to a couple of girls, and they came over. I repeated Joan's question and said, "Girls, let's make a huddle here for privacy," and we put our arms around each other's shoulders.

I prayed, "Thank You, Lord Jesus, that *You love Joan*. Thank You, for loving her *just as she is*." As I stopped, in that split second, from the corner of my eye, I saw tears dripping from her nose! With a little pressure on her shoulder, I said, "Joan, you tell Him, too." She did, with more tears, and suddenly the huddle broke up and her face was filled with light!

That evening before I retired, I sought her out and asked her how she was doing. "Oh, Ros, I feel like a horse who has done a day's work!" And she laughed, and then immediately turning to a friend sitting by her, "Ros, this is Genny. She needs just what's happened to me today."

I said, "Hi, Genny. . . ." and stopped. In that quick second, Genny had put her head down on the table and there were more tears! Looking up at Joan, I said, "Let's take her off into a little huddle, shall we?" And we did.

The next morning at breakfast I learned that after lights went out in that particular room, open-hearted prayers were offered one by one. I also learned that Genny had wept quietly in her own upper bunk for more than two hours. The woman who told me stayed awake, too, to keep a vigil of love and faith with her.

I told this story in a certain church sometime later and a comment came back to me: "Miss Rinker doesn't teach people to repent!" Repent? What was Genny doing those two hours in the dark, weeping her heart out? And who taught her to do that? Rosalind Rinker? No, the Holy Spirit Himself, the faithful Guide and Teacher and Comforter. Who can teach better than He? There are many things He does much better than I (understatement of the year) and more and more I am content to let Him do it. All He seems to put in my heart is to tell the story over and over: *God loves you. God loves you just as you are!*

I've heard from both Joan and Genny, and I want to share a few paragraphs of Genny's letter:

"Every night I thank God for that conference. What a change in my life, my whole family in fact! For years I've been searching. I took a year of instruction in the .... Church, but that didn't seem to be for me. When you started talking, I felt at once I was near to what I'd been seeking for all those years. Then I was afraid I wasn't going to get to talk to you. Had I only known, I didn't have to worry. God saw to it, since it was my time to meet Him.

"When I got in the car to go home, I knew I should tell my husband, Jack, right away, and the longer I put it off, the harder it got. So I said a little prayer and started right in. Jack thought it was a wonderful idea to have prayer in our home every night — we've only missed three nights so far. The kids remind us if we forget!

"So many wonderful things have happened to us and for us. We come so much closer to each other. The children's grades have gone from C's and D's to A's and B's. Our twelve-year-old even says a little prayer when he plays football. None of us do anything now without first saying a little prayer — it's so easy then.

"After that wonderful thing happened to me, I wondered if this was the new life, the rebirth. I prayed about it, and immediately the answer came in Genie Price's book, *What Is God Like?* It was almost like God read my mind! I know now, and thank Him with tears of joy. I'm the happiest I've ever been in my life, and therefore my family is happy."

You can start where you are, quietly and simply, by giving thanks to Jesus Christ for what He has given you. If you cannot yet bring yourself to ask another to "give thanks" with you, pray alone but do pray audibly. Thank Him for everything. This is your response to His giving and His gifts. Your response means He will be able to continue to reach to you, to speak to you, to communicate with you, as He did with Genny.

Even if you sometimes fail to respond, He is faithful and continues to be faithful according to His own unchanging nature, waiting until you are ready to respond and to receive with a thankful heart both the Gift and particularly the Giver.

Giving thanks is a sign of the Responsive Heart.

Sayings of the heart

Gratitude is illumination.
Gratitude is the form of a smiling mind.
Gratitude is the pulse of a singing heart.
Gratitude is the root of love.
Gratitude is singing balance in all the body.
Gratitude is the dawn of joy.
Gratitude is the great and ready peace of being a man.
Gratitude is our welcome to all the world.
Gratitude reveals great meanings in our day, in our doing, in our sudden joy.
Gratitude is the sacred awakening of our consonance with God.
Gratitude is our rejoicing and our song of Heart.
Gratitude is our great affirmation of life.
Gratitude is the region of spirit in which we may dwell.
Gratitude is our home in the presence of God.

ROBERT RAYNOLDS*

*From *In Praise of Gratitude* (Harper, pp. 18, 19).

For Discussion

1. What new discovery did the author make, through the experiences of Mary Ann, Joan and Genny?
2. Share what you have learned regarding the importance of gratitude from this chapter. What conditions must be met?
3. What other questions might add to the practical application of this subject?

Prayer Time

Silently With pencil and paper, make a list of the things and people for which you are thankful . . . remember the Giver of all good things.

Audibly If you have never participated in audible prayer why not do it today? A sincere, simple thankful sentence will begin to open your heart and set you free. Even if another expresses it before you get around to it — say it, pray it — because it is yours, and comes from your heart.

5

Can God Love You? two stories

In our last chapter we thought about the power of gratitude which can sometimes bridge the gap between a man and his God. Who can know what the Holy Spirit may have said to any one of those persons before the first audible prayer: "Thank You, Lord, for loving me." One person kept adding, "for loving *even me, even me.*" The sense of unworthiness and the fear of not being loved and accepted by God is an acute one; herein the roots of repentance. I've witnessed the acute struggle which goes on before that first vocal prayer, and believe me, it's not always due to pride or fear of the sound of their own voices.

When a man is faced with the Presence of Jesus Christ, and has chosen to speak to Him from his heart, where does he start? There are many *ways* to start and God hears them all; but there is only one *place* to start and that's the place of repentance — even though the person may not be aware of its name.

Did you ever consider that giving thanks can be a way of showing your repentant heart? Let me ask you first, is any one sin worse than another in God's sight? which do you consider the greatest, if we can dare to classify sin? All sin is sin in God's eyes: missing the mark He has set for us, going our own way instead of His way. His way will bring health and peace and life — while ours can do just the opposite. In the first chapter of Romans, Paul tells us that the greatest sin is unthankfulness—not knowing, not recognizing and not giving thanks to God.

Think of all the good things of life freely given to each one of us for which we have never been thankful. Think of God loving each one of us, just as we are, because He knows our potential in Him — and we've never had the courtesy or the time or the inclination to say, *Thank You, God.* If this realization has ever come over you, you'll be so overwhelmed that you won't be able to label your feelings for quite a while. You will just want to cry out of your repentant heart (that wants to change and to stop being ungrateful), "Oh, Lord, *how could You* love me!" That's what repentance is.

Think of Christ on the cross providing forgiveness for you, and you've never personally thanked Him! Never thanked Him for the gift of forgiveness, never thanked Him for the injustice, the rejection and tragedy He suffered to make this gift possible. Never thanked Him that He, being the Giver, is Himself the Gift! Isn't the realization of this kind of ingratitude the beginning of true repentance?

Repentance is used by Christ in stating His purpose and is defined in *The Amplified New Testament.*

> *. . . Jesus came into Galilee, preaching the good news (the Gospel) of the kingdom of God, And saying, The* [*appointed period of*] *time is (completed) fulfilled, and the kingdom of God is at hand; repent (have a change of mind which issues in regret for past sins and in change of conduct for the better) and believe — trust in, rely on and adhere to the good news — the Gospel* (Mark 1: 14, 15, *Amplified*).

Repentance was not even in my vocabulary when I found Christ at fifteen years of age (chapter 6). I only knew I needed Him and wanted Him. I've done more repenting during the years I've been a Christian than I ever did at the time of my conversion. I did have a change of mind, I began to want to do God's will instead of my own. Isn't this real repentance as Jesus defined it?

I've been watching the transformation which comes when it dawns on people that God really loves them. I've been joyfully sharing what I've seen. And yet — some good soul who listens will afterward take me aside (it happened two weeks ago) and say, "Dear, when were *you* converted? Don't *you* preach repentance and confession for salvation?" In the case just mentioned, I said to her minister, "Does that good sister *love* people?" He smiled, "Well, she talks about it, but she's pretty hard on them!"

In my experience, repentance with real sorrow, with weeping and regret over the past, does not come easily to the average person — as it comes to the skid-row person at the time of conversion. He's down and out and he knows it. The average Mr. and Mrs. America has an unfilled void, a need; they can't quite believe a holy God could or would love an unholy person. Not that repentance cannot be realized as such. God meets us where we are, and gets into the first crack in our armor, and believe me, He'll get into any little opening that's there!

I want to tell you about several people in this chapter. One young woman seemed (to the Christians) to have a very repentant heart, and yet, wait until you see what was giving her all the agony! The other, a man who prayed his first audible sentence, "breaking the sound barrier" in a group of like-minded people, couldn't even remember what he said. Yet, he was powerfully converted and his life has been a living testimony ever since. Then he found someone who remembered what he had prayed. There is a false repentance and a true repentance; all that meets the human eye is not always valid. Only God knows what is going on, and sometimes we must wait and know them by their fruits. Thus do we begin to become acquainted with the ways of God in human hearts — the ways of love and of holy wooing.

The Story of Charlotte

Introduction: This young woman came to her counselor in great distress for help and understanding.

Charlotte: I've been a Christian for two years, and something's wrong, my Christian life just isn't working right.

Counselor: What do you mean, not working right?

Charlotte: I don't enjoy prayer; I have to *make* myself read my Bible and go to church, and — well, isn't that enough?

Counselor: Suppose you tell me how you entered the Door — how you came to Christ?

Charlotte: There isn't much to tell. A friend took me to some special church services, and I felt I ought to be a Christian. For a whole week I had a terrible struggle — I couldn't eat or sleep.

Counselor: What were you struggling about? Would you like to tell me?

Charlotte: Oh yes, I'll never forget it! If I accepted the ways of the Christians, and gave up the worldly ways this church preached against — what would my parents think? What would all my friends think? After a week of this agony, I made my decision. I would become a Christian and accept their ways.

Counselor: Did you find peace then?

Charlotte: Yes, for a while — until things began to pile up. But I *never* seem to know what's right and what isn't, and I never seem to be able to find God's will, nor hear Him speaking to me.

Counselor: (After a quiet moment) I have one question I'd like to have you think about: Where does *Jesus Christ* come into this picture? You didn't mention Him once.

Charlotte: I didn't? No-o, I guess I didn't, did I? I guess I just took Him for granted.

Counselor: Your true decision is: to belong to Christ

or *not* to belong to Christ. All the other do's and don'ts come later. As His child, you will be guided, and there will be growth and peace instead of doubt and confusion.

Charlotte: That's what I want. I want to belong to Jesus Christ and let Him run my life.

Closing Comment: This young woman "belonged" to the church people and their opinions. Now she has experienced true repentance for her sins, including spiritual blindness which kept Christ outside for so long. Now she is growing as a Christian should, and knows to whom she belongs.

The Story of Dave

Dave is a great big friendly fellow with a crew cut. The one thorn in his flesh was that his wife was a beautiful Christian, while he couldn't see what she was so excited about. He went to church; he'd been confirmed, why — he even taught a Sunday school class. Yet, the sincerity and reality of Thelma's walk with God got under his skin. Finally he was willing to go with her several hundred miles to a Faith at Work Conference and see what this was all about.

The open-hearted testimonies of God's power to change dispositions, situations, and lives held his attention. But the joy and the holy laughter and freedom of the people made him mad because he seemed to be on the outside and he didn't know how to get in.

One of his friends shared his predicament with some of us, and asked us to pray for him. "Dave's just told his wife she's gone too far this time — bringing him here with all these fanatical people! He's gone for his car, and is driving back home alone. Is he mad! But that's a good sign too, isn't it?" Dave didn't leave, he couldn't leave, God's love is never more powerful than when it is holding us unconditionally.

I heard the whole story six months later when he and his wife came to the airport to meet me.

Thelma: Oh, Ros, is my husband ever changed! He's like a new man!

Ros: Is that so! I want to hear about it. When did it happen?

Thelma: Let *him* tell you when he brings the car around, he'd love to tell it himself.

Here's Dave's own story:

"You know . . . at that conference, I couldn't even back the car out . . . I turned on the engine, let it run, then turned it off. I just sat there. I knew I couldn't go home. Then, Ros, Hal took me into your prayer group, remember? When I heard your simple instruction on prayer, I wanted to pray, but I couldn't. That night, after Gert Behanna spoke, you gave some more instruction on prayer, remember? (I remembered, it was an extra meeting for people who wanted help in audible prayer.) I stayed, and determined that if it killed me, I'd pray aloud if you gave us a chance. It seemed like my only hope, my only chance.

"And you did give us time to pray—sentence prayers—giving thanks—or whatever we wanted to say. I remember you saying: 'Make it right from your heart, and speak directly to the Lord Jesus.' Well, I sweated it out, and finally made it! I prayed aloud. And it seemed like God was right there. After that, you had us make little cups out of our hands while we were in the attitude and spirit of prayer, so the Lord Jesus could fill them full of His love and all the good things He had for us. That's all I remember, and that's all I did. But, boy, was I changed! And everything and everybody seemed changed, too! Since I've come back, I want to tell everybody to pray, to get face-to-face with Jesus Christ."

I asked Dave what he said when he prayed that sentence prayer, and with a shrug of his shoulders he said he couldn't remember, and did it matter?

Later that week, a young married woman was relating how faith and new life in Christ came to her. "It was when I heard Dave pray at that instruction meeting you gave us, that everything hit me! I went back to my room, got into my bunk, and prayed and wept for about four hours. Oh, I was such a sinner!"

When she finished her story, I asked her what Dave prayed, and as she remembered it, here it is: "Lord Jesus, thank You for loving a stubborn old sinner like me." So there you have it — a thank you-prayer, and a repentant-prayer all at once. A thankful heart can be a repentant heart, all in one man at the same time.

The miracle of spiritual life took place in that instant, as Dave spoke to Jesus Christ; he knew he was accepted and loved.

"When does life begin?" I asked a group of college students from the University of Wisconsin. "At birth" came the ready answer. I waited a moment, watching them, and saw the truth break on Max's face. "Well," he said, "if there isn't any life before birth, it's too late, isn't it?"

Physically speaking, it takes nine months for a new baby to be born. Spiritually speaking, who is to say how long it takes? You'll only know after it happens to you. Each one is different. In each person, God's love and God's Spirit are preparing the heart, making the heart receptive — over a period of time, by many and varied means.

One thing remains constant — a truly repentant heart is always a responsive heart.

> *So repent — change your mind and purpose; turn around and return* [to God], *that your sins may be erased (blotted out, wiped clean), that times of refreshing . . . may come from the presence of the Lord* (Acts 3:19, *Amplified*).

For Discussion

1. How is the whole idea of repentance developed here?
2. Study its beginnings, its roots, its scope, its expression.
3. Underline all that is pertinent to linking God's love with repentance.
4. Discuss the ideas of false and true repentance, as they affected the lives of Charlotte and Dave.

Prayer Time

Silently Meditate, think, and pray on the underlined material in No. 3 above.

Audibly Pray in simple sentences (not paragraphs) so that many may pray several times, giving *thanks* or *asking*, as the heart-need may indicate.

6

The Impatient Heart: a college professor

> . . . *ye are God's husbandry* . . . (I Corinthians 3:9, KJV).
>
> *You are God's farmland.* . . . (I Corinthians 3:9, *Berkeley*).
>
> . . . *you are God's garden and vineyard and field under cultivation.* . . . (I Corinthians 3:9, *Amplified*).
>
> . . . *you are a field under God's cultivation.* . . . (I Corinthians 3:9, *Phillips*).

IN EACH OF THE ABOVE translations, from I Corinthians 3:9 the Apostle Paul's teaching becomes increasingly meaningful. Your heart is likened to a plot of ground, but you don't own it, nor do you cultivate it. You are under cultivation; you are being worked-over, prepared by God through the influences He has been and is now sending into your life.

Jesus gives us further light on this subject in the parable of the sower who went out to sow the seed which fell into four kinds of ground. No matter which kind of soil may be predominant in any heart, if we have ears to hear, we can begin to get rid of the rocks, weed out the thorns, break up and soften the hard soil; thus preparing our hearts to be receptive and ready for the seed, that life-giving message, the Word, Christ Himself.

Now if you noticed, I have just succeeded in contradicting myself in those two first paragraphs. In the first one, I said you neither owned nor cultivated your plot of ground, in the second one I said you could at least do the latter. However, I suggested in the first paragraph a passivity that permits outside influences to determine what happens in order to shape you up. I also suggested that the positive, good, caring influences of God, your Heavenly Father, was present, because He happens to care about the property which He created.

In the second paragraph, please notice, no matter what kind of soil the plot may have, there is hope. For Jesus said, *He who has ears to hear, let him hear* (Luke 8:8). We can do something about the condition of our hearts, providing we can hear. In other words, what if there is dry hard ground, or rocks and thorns, if you have ears and respond — you can begin to do something. You can begin to foster a state of receptivity within your plot of ground.

However, if you cannot hear, then is it because you have no ears? No response mechanism which is operating? He who will not hear, cannot be changed (Luke 8:9, 10).

He who has ears to hear, can expect cultivation to begin. God cares so much that He longs for your response. Only in the cooperative effort of love responding to invitation, is there dynamic sufficient for change. "When the powerful, drawing, magnetic love of God begins to move upon a human heart, that heart becomes responsive." The resulting receptivity prepares the heart for the deep ploughing, the harrowing, the seeding, the weeding, the watering, and the growing.

The prepared heart may appear to be quiet and peaceful; only God knows the depths to which any person is brought before he surrenders to Christ.

Some years ago, during a week in which I participated in a Faith at Work Conference in a certain state, I met such "a prepared heart." C.S., hearing of the conference, came to meet the author of a book on prayer that had helped her.

Mrs. M., the pastor's wife, brought C.S. to me one afternoon and introduced us. When I heard why she had come, there was a strange moving within me of God's Spirit toward her. Knowing absolutely nothing at all about her, I took her hand and led her into one of the adjoining Sunday school rooms where we could have a few moments of privacy.

We sat down. I remember taking both her hands in mine, and starting to give thanks in prayer . . . without any further word of conversation. Again I felt the great moving love of God within me. In great waves, that all-knowing, all-encompassing love of God seemed to break all around the two of us. I knew this one whom I had just met, was known and loved by God. The expression of this seemed to pour out of me as if it were being poured into me! Which indeed it was!

As I recall, of such tenderness and of such magnitude was this revealing of God's love in Christ, that tears flowed unheeded, as if the very tears themselves were part of the overflowing love.

C.S. also joined in this expression with gratefulness and thankfulness that she was a participant and receiver of such love. That evening, she and her husband attended a group discussion, and she shared the fresh revelation of God which had been given to her that day and called it her rebirth.

Here, once again, I witnessed the power of God's Spirit reaching to a responsive heart. She was a prepared heart. All we did was to give thanks, offer praise, and worship Him together there in that Sunday school room. Those of you who have already read the chapter entitled Can God Love You?, will be prepared to understand this miracle. For it was a miracle. "Every time God's love in Christ is revealed to a receptive heart, it is a fresh miracle."

C.S. and I have corresponded since then. I've learned that she and her husband are university professors who have sought by many and varied roads the peace of God. When I knew I was going to write this book, I wanted to include her — for hers was one of the most prepared hearts I've ever encountered.

What had God previously done to prepare "her plot of ground"? I'd never asked her. What has He done since? She never told me until I asked her to share a few of the revelations, insights, and knowledge which have come to her — both before and since that time.

Here is the story, told in her own words:

"You ask me how I feel God had prepared me for what happened March 16, 1962 . . . what I want to say and what I shall eventually say will be far short of my goal. I've asked myself that question many times, and tonight before I started to write, it finally struck me that I've never been conscious that God was preparing me for anything! Only now, as I look back and begin to write, am I really aware of how great His love has been and how somehow He is using everything that ever happened to me to show me how much He loves me.

"As a child, I had a strong sense of Jesus, but lost it in my teens; then, after marriage, divorce and remarriage with all the accompanying suffering, I also lost (by death) many who were near and dear to me. I, too, seemed lost, until last year when I was re-born.

"In case you want the basic biological facts: I have had two careers, in the field of radio, as Dramatic Director, and in Sociology. My husband is a Ph.D. in Economics, and after 25 years of teaching at various colleges and universities, has retired to write; but something is happening in him, too. God is with him, and will help him decide what the next step is to be.

"My first God-consciousness came around six years of age. I should say, I was conscious of Jesus through His mother, Mary. As a Catholic I was taught that if one prayed to Mary and asked her to intercede for you to her Son, one would be granted anything. So I 'fell in love' with Jesus at a very early age.

"Being the fourth youngest of five children, with an Italian background, there was very close relationship both to the church and to a very large family of aunts, uncles, cousins, and in-laws, and grandparents whose letters from Italy influenced the whole tribe of us. It is small wonder I didn't get crushed with all these people I had to go through in order to reach to Jesus. As a result, I turned inward and decided I'd find Jesus *on my own*. And I did. I received Holy Communion at six — I loved to receive Communion. I felt very, very close to Jesus. He was very real to me. I remember the hymn that was sung by the choir as I walked down the aisle to receive Communion — I can hear it still, 'Oh, Lord, I am not worthy, that Thou shouldst come to me.' After the wafer touched my tongue I felt extremely worthy for a few moments, but the confessional (which preceded communion) never made me feel cleansed, and I'll tell you why.

"We had to go through soul-searching for the minutest of sins. (I say this with humility, so help me God, because of how different my later years were.) After a few times of going to confession, I realized I didn't have any sins to confess: I didn't lie to my parents, I didn't steal, I didn't call my girl friends bad names, I didn't quarrel with my brothers and sisters. I didn't tell dirty stories. If I ever said a swear word, I always repeated, 'God forgive me.' I'm certain the reason I didn't indulge in these sins was not because of my extreme innocence; it was due to my fear of hell, which the church succeeded in instilling in me at a young age. All I can say in defense of my seeming purity was that I was scared to death of burning in hell! For me there was only one way to salvation — that was *not to sin*, and sin I didn't.

"One day, a few years later, it occurred to me that I couldn't possibly be *that* pure, so I decided that I must be committing sins and didn't know it. I corrected that by lying to the priest; I *had to,* if I wanted to receive Communion. I'd invent sins, venial sins. Later on I concluded to myself 'C......, you're not this good; but if you are, all I can say for you is that some day you're going to be a terrible sinner. Maybe God is helping you be ready for those sins, by not sinning now.' Wasn't I a conceited little egotist? It was true . . . later, much later.

"Call it God, call it fear, call it what you will. I was determined as a child that I would be saved! At a mission I heard that if one received Communion for nine consecutive first Fridays of each month, no matter what one did in later years, this act was enough to see them through to salvation. I grasped this wonderful knowledge and became determined to go through with this experience. It wasn't easy for a child of ten to go to confession the night before, go early to mass without breakfast, then to Communion, and then to school. But I did it, all on my own. My mother was not one to discuss this sort of thing; if she had known of my fears and doubts, she would have claimed I was bad, bad, bad. She was very close to the church, but lacked real understanding of religion. Dad was not so close, but had the real thing.

"I don't ever remember discussing my love for Jesus with anyone in the family. I continued to work my way to Jesus and God *all alone,* and I loved doing it. One day I conquered a fear all by myself. I was beginning to question Catholicism by now. I'd had a hearty breakfast, and suddenly I had a strong urge to receive Communion. How could I without going to confession, and I'd eaten breakfast! I prayed to God for guidance. I felt He urged me to get up and go to the rail and receive Communion. I did. Walking back I felt clean, and wasn't surprised that He didn't strike me dead.

"Because of my doubts I started calling on my priest

for weekly sessions. I wanted to know more about the reality of God. He spoke freely and told me things that startled me. One day I said, 'Father, why don't you preach this way from the altar? More people would listen.' He replied, 'My dear, I can't, but I speak to you this way because I know you won't take advantage of what I tell you.' Little did he know of the dangerous weapon he handed me right there and then.

"The next visit I put it straight. 'Father,' I said, 'Jesus what is this God-business all about?' He replied, 'My dear, God is either very, very forgiving, or we are all of us going to hell.'

"That did it. I walked away thinking, *So that's it, eh? I don't have a thing to worry about. We're all in the same boat.* I never went back. I felt free, secure, and very complacent. I felt I had gone to the highest authority I knew of at that time seeking knowledge. I got it, so I could go on my merry way. God would take care of me no matter what I did.

"The surprising thing about my acts of rebellion (as the church would call them) was that I didn't feel rebellious, a sense of peace would pervade my whole being. My experimenting with Jesus and God continued until my sophomore year in college when I knew I had to make a decision for or against God — not really God as I look back now — but Catholicism. I married in the church, but never went again for fifteen years.

"After my marriage, I thought science had the answer, and followed the lead of my husband. I never do things in half measure. During those twelve black years, flaunting my scientific know-how in teaching and in my social life, I forgot every prayer I ever learned, except the 'Our Father.' During the long period of suffering that came during our divorce, I tried to pray by repeating 'Our Father' over and over; I tried by prayer to find out if divorce was the right thing for us, and prayed that we both might find God.

"During this period of agony, I remembered a pact I had made with Jesus in my teens. One day in church, feeling extremely close to Him, I made a vow. 'Dear sweet Jesus, I love You so much I want to know the whole truth; for Your sake I'm willing to experience everything You ever suffered, providing You teach me the truth.' You didn't have to take me so literal. Please spare me now.' Well, He didn't. (At least, not until that morning I committed myself to Him with you, Ros. Do you see now why God had to let that morning come to me?)

"Then the divorce went through, my husband remarried . . . and so did I. My first husband died of a heart attack, and I went to pieces. I thought all my praying was in vain, I felt truly abandoned by God then. I thought He hadn't heard my prayers. Why didn't He let him live, and be touched by God as I was beginning to be touched?

"After his death, with all of my hatred and self-pity, I tried to reach God. I vowed that I'd get to Him again. Then I realized I could only do it by learning to love Jesus as I did when a child. I prayed to Him constantly for five years. (God sent a son into our lives whom we love very much.) My husband with all of his problems, was trying to find God again. God has been very, very good to me. I don't know why. Ten years ago I tried to reach God by writing a book about Him. Some joke! I had a long, long way to go yet. And still I must keep on. I wrote many of my experiences down, in an attempt to understand what God was doing in my life. I wrote my prayers down, I wrote poems trying to show how through all of my doubts, wrongdoing and rebellions, I continued in a lame fashion to work for God, though I didn't seem to get very far.

"Since being recommitted to Christ on an adult plane, I have lost my fears. I know I am on the right path. I feel like a child again, when I believed in utter simplicity and innocence, but with a grown-up mind. How wonderful! How sweet! How all encompassing! How complete it all is!

"Five months after my conversion, I wrote this letter:

"Dear Lord,

"Teach me over and over again wherein I err. Keep me ever mindful of my wrongdoings, rather than those of my brothers, blaming myself, not them. Do not hesitate to point up in sharp perspective what I am truly like, for I must know me as I am in Your sight before I can change. How can I do this without Your Divine help? Alone I am utterly helpless and crushed. Show me, Lord, how to make my weaknesses my strength.

"Lord, teach me Thy ways so that I may know without a doubt when I am serving Mammon and when I am serving You. There are so many ways that Satan tempts me, and it is difficult to know 'who is who.' If I knew for certain, I would be able to do Your will with ease and serenity. But it's in this not knowing for certain that I need Your help most.

"I know I am new in Your service. It is only five months since I committed myself to You through Rosalind Rinker. Am I expecting too much too soon? If so, I confess my sin of impatience, an impatience due solely to an aching need of You. This ache is so great that my whole being pains with anguish to have you near me for solace."

Many people who know C.S. think of her as a person who has not been touched by life. If they only knew what depths she had to go before peace came to her. There are many things which happened during her stage of preparation that belong only to her and to Jesus.

She requested this chapter be titled, "The Impatient Heart," so eager is she to learn more, to experience more of God. It was with mixed emotions that she finally consented to write from her own experiences. They are included now, with a prayer for the person reading them who feels that the dark years are too dark, that there is no way Home. There is. There is a Way.

Just as the great Father-heart of God prepared C.S. in her early life, to love Jesus, and remember later; so He has given you something to remember. It will come to you. You will recall His early caring for you. The ground can be broken up, the rocks and the thorns removed, and the heart made receptive and responsive. If there is not one single thing you can recall, then what about this one chapter. What about the fact that your eyes lit on this chapter, and you read it? God is in this. This is His love telling you there is hope. And where there's hope, there is also faith — and love.

God's love reaching to your responding heart.

For Discussion

1. What is the contradiction in the first three paragraphs?
2. What new meanings do the words "a prepared heart" take on, as a result of reading this chapter.
3. Talk together about "prepared hearts" among people you are constantly meeting.

Prayer Time

Silently read the last two paragraphs.
Recall God's early caring for you.
Think on the fact of His never-changing love.
Dwell on His unconditional love for you.
Permit God's love to invade your responding heart.

Audibly Do what your hearts tell you to do.
Never be afraid of silence. God is there.
Always give thanks.

7

God Loves a Rebel: a normal delinquent

> *I have let myself be sought out by those who did not inquire for Me; I was found by those who did not seek Me. I said: Here am, I,* HERE AM *I, to a nation which did not call on My name. I spread forth My hands all day long to a rebellious people, who walk in a way which is not good, after their own devices* (Isaiah 65:1, 2, *Berkeley*).

"I THINK I'VE BEEN A REBEL all my life. Questioning, trying to find out why, looking for something that made sense, searching for a philosophy of life." Sandra, not yet 21, tall, slender, feels that life handed her more than her share right from the start.

An only child, she learned early that she was an adopted child. Where were her own parents? Didn't they love her? Didn't anyone really love her? Why did she always get the blunt end of everything?

"I couldn't even finish high school like a normal kid. True, I was an officer in my class and a member of the basketball team — but I broke a light bulb. For this, two months later I was kicked out of school and told never to come back, so my mother sent me to night school at the Y. and I worked during the day.

"There must be some reason for things as they are," Sandy tried to explain, "there must be a God but He doesn't seem to care for me. Then I thought the answer could be the mind of man, but if it were, why hasn't he found out something by this time? So I decided I'd be a normal juvenile delinquent and go my own normal way, and not worry about anyone else!

What aggravated me most was that some people seemed happy and I wasn't. I tried to be polite to them, but I couldn't. In my heart I'm just a rebel!"

Then Sandy, now a medical technician, met several Christians. For almost two months she asked questions. What is God like? What is prayer? Will God hear me if I pray?

She began reading for herself, asking more questions, and praying quietly in her heart. Several years ago, Sandy rejected religion altogether because its theological dogmatism seemed to leave no room for her to think for herself. Then, a young woman who was a Christian, was hospitalized, needed blood tests from Sandy's laboratory — and there was another contact.

"In that hospital room, I saw love in action. The love Christians have for each other," said Sandra. And to herself, she said, "These people have something I want." She demands a lot of life, she has a great capacity for love, and came dangerously close to being a disillusioned perfectionist at the age of 20. Jesus said it would work like this: "By loving one another, all men shall know you are my disciples" (John 13:34, 35). Hope came to Sandra, as it comes to all, through Christ and the love He has for us and gives us for each other. Only by loving one another can we survive.

One evening she was speaking of all these things with still another Christian friend, who finally said to her, "Jesus is right here, Sandy. Why not give yourself to Him? Here. Now."

There was a small silence and a deep quietness. Then ". . . I did it! I gave myself to Him." With the realization that she had really given herself, and was accepted by Christ, she seemed to possess fresh powers to express all the love and belonging that was filling her heart.

"I gave myself to Him, and *He loves me,* stinker that I am. He's my God now, not just your God, or Dickie's, or Lorrie's. He's *my* God. He loves *me.* And

He loves everybody! Why . . . He's been here all the time, hasn't He, and I never recognized Him before."

The overflowing joy of discovering that God loved her, that He loves everyone, sent Sandy to the telephone to call several friends and tell them, too. With each telling, the wonder increased. God's love. His forgiveness. His acceptance of her. A new purpose began to take hold in her heart, the whole world was new. She not only was loved, she discovered that she loved everyone.

She discovered how much her parents loved her.

She wanted everyone she worked with, technicians, doctors, nurses, and the elevator operators, to know that God loved her and that He loves them.

"The wonder of it all is that this is not me as I know me!" she tried to explain. "The whole world is filled with God and He loves us all! Why didn't someone tell me before?"

She might as well ask, why didn't that lily bloom last week? Or why wasn't the baby born next week? When it's time for life to come forth, nothing can hold it back. The heart of this little rebel was tender and receptive. She only made it appear that she was callous, hard and unresponsive, to protect herself. But hoping against hope, she kept searching because a loving God kept making her heart receptive, more receptive than she knew.

The bravado of the rebel slipped away from her like an unwanted garment. Suddenly she was taught of God from within, the personal quality of His love amazed her. Immediately His love filled her, flowing down into her own responsive, prepared, hungry heart, and immediately she was giving it away to everyone who would listen.

It's not the rebellious heart that causes the most concern, it's the disillusioned heart. The rebel is protesting, that very protest being a sign of the deep interest within. The disillusioned one has lost hope, if he ever had any. Apathy is a difficult adversary. But there is nothing too difficult for God, because there is nothing too difficult for His quality of love.

God's love is like the sun in Aesop's fable. The sun and the wind had an argument over who was the strongest. They decided that the test would be, who could make a certain man take off his coat. The wind, with all his huffing and puffing failed; the sun, with his penetrating warmth soon succeeded.

God's love isn't like man's love — there is no discrimination nor differentiation in God's love. Most people do not love a rebel. God does. He gives to them the same fresh air, green earth, lovely sunsets, gorgeous flowers, bread and butter that He gives to the faithful. He knows their searching hearts, He knows what will make them respond, and He knows the spring planting from the autumn harvest.

God *does care* what happens, and He has done something about it. Jesus told us that even though five sparrows were sold for one nickel, yet not one of them is forgotten in God's sight. He even told us the very hairs on our heads are all numbered! Rejoicing is the keynote of the fifteenth chapter of Luke, with Jesus' graphic stories of the lost sheep, the lost coin and the lost son. "Rejoice with me! My son was lost and is found!"

The lost son was first a rebel who left everything to go "his own normal delinquent way." Later on, after he had made a complete mess of his life and sat in the pig-sty, hopelessly hungry and filthy, a ray of hope suddenly came to him. He would go home to his father!

This lost son began to take the first steps homeward before he ever moved out of that pig-sty. He talked to himself, his real self hidden away down underneath; he talked to God, whom he had ignored. He just poured it all out — he was hungry, thirsty, dirty; he was bankrupt in every area, ashamed of himself, sick and tired of everyone else, and totally bored with having no purpose in life. He was suddenly homesick. He wanted to go home. His father would understand, his father would accept him.

Have you pursued goals that have left you a hopeless shadow of what you once thought you could be? Make up your mind to go home, but first talk to yourself! Put everything you feel into words, rant and rave if necessary, against everything and everyone — get it out of your system. God is there, He understands. Then ask forgiveness. As you do this you'll discover *He is there,* and you are moving toward Him. Your verbal outbreak will do one of two things. Either you will break down and weep bitter, cleansing tears, or you will laugh aloud with joy as you see through your futility and realize you are on your way home.

"Your Father in heaven is waiting for you, loving you. He has everything prepared for you. He loves you just as you are, because He knows what He's going to do for you. He knows your real potential."

When you've found Christ as your Saviour, you're at home. When you've found God as your Father, you're at home. Your heart will know. To be at home is to be where He is, to be free to accept His love, and to love Him in return. Free to trust His wisdom when life seems contradictory. It doesn't seem to matter so much because His love is great enough. He will carry out His purpose for you. To begin with, all you need to do to help Him is to love Him and trust Him.

When you are willing to respond to Him, no rebellion is too big for His love.

For Discussion

1. How is God's love different from human love?
2. Discuss the value of open rebellion in contrast to secret rebellion.
3. Do you know any rebels? How would Jesus greet them?

Prayer Time

Silently Accept God's love, for yourself. He is interested in *now*. Accept God's love for one who is a rebel. Find ways to communicate this love.

Audibly Pray together, for each other by name, and for others not present.

8

God Loves Them (your relatives)

> *Son, your sins are forgiven . . .* (Mark 2:5, *Amplified*).
>
> *And to her He said, Your sins are forgiven* (Luke 7:48, *Berkeley*).

A PARALYZED MAN was placed in front of Jesus, by the combined efforts of four men who had to tear a hole in the roof to let him down. They knew Jesus could make him walk again. To their great surprise and dismay, they could hardly believe their ears when they heard Jesus say, "Son, your sins are forgiven." I can almost hear one of those four bearers of the stretcher remonstrate and say, "But Master, we brought him to You for healing!"

A little later, Jesus said words to this effect, "Which do you think is easier for Me to do, heal a man's body or heal his soul?" Then to prove His point to those whose hearts were filled with unbelief, He said, "To let you know that the Son of Man has power to forgive sins on the earth," here He turned to the paralyzed man, "I tell you rise, pick up your mat and go home." They were all amazed and glorified God, saying, "We never yet saw anything like it!"

Only Jesus knew the real reason for the paralysis. Only Jesus could go to the source. He did, without any apology, or introduction, or reasons why. I wonder how long that man had carried his load of guilt? How much was his, and how much had others contributed to it? What hardness of heart, isolation of spirit, and inner torment had been his companions day and night?

Then Jesus spoke to him, "*Son, your sins are forgiven.*"

I once saw two men carry into the church a lady who was completely paralyzed. Though she was as stiff as a board, she could hear perfectly and wanted to come to the meeting. Later I learned that she lived with her sister whom she hated, because the parents left the bulk of the fortune to one and not to the other! Her paralysis was a form of arthritis, an emotionally induced disease, resulting from deep feelings of injustice, self-pity, unforgiveness and hatred. She hated her parents for leaving her a pittance; she hated her sister for possessing more than she — and she could forgive none of them, either for what they did, or for what they were.

Three years later I heard the joyous news. She had been completely restored to health! Through the miracle of prayer and forgiveness, her sins had been forgiven, and she had forgiven those whom she felt had wronged her. Paralyzing poison had nothing to feed upon. She regained full use of her whole body.

> *For if you forgive others their trespasses, your heavenly Father will forgive you, too; but if you do not forgive people, neither will your heavenly Father forgive your trespasses* (Matthew 6:14, 15, *Berkeley*).

Jesus is not driving a hard bargain here, and saying that if you will forgive others, then you, too, can be forgiven. He is merely stating a principle of the Kingdom: hardness of heart which is a result of unforgiveness will automatically prevent God from forgiving your sins. When I withhold forgiveness from my brother for any reason, I prevent God's forgiveness from getting through to me. Someone effectively points out that until God gives me His kind of Love, I am unable to forgive. This is true. It's sort of a balanced circle, isn't it? If I want God's forgiveness, what right do I have to hold something against my brother and refuse him my forgiveness?

After Eugenia Price had been a guest in the home

of a dear friend of mine, the friend said to me, "Genie helped me with a great, big problem."

I asked if she would mind telling me about it. "Not at all," was the reply. "You see, I have an only brother. Our parents are dead, so naturally, he means a great deal to me. Recently, he married for the second time and his present wife doesn't seem to care about coming to our home. I'm developing a strong feeling of dislike for her. And it's growing into proportions I can't handle. I actually don't like her — I can't forgive her for what is happening between my brother and me. She's driving our family apart."

"What did Genie tell you?" I prompted her.

"She simply asked me one question, 'Did it ever occur to you that God loves that sister-in-law as much as He loves you?' That did it. By remembering how much God loves her, I was soon able to love and to forgive her."

> *Be kind to each other, be understanding. Be as ready to forgive others as God for Christ's sake has forgiven you* (Ephesians 4:32, *Phillips*).

Human unforgiveness stems from roots of personal injury. Who possesses a sufficient supply of the milk of human kindness, to forgive either enemies, or those whom one despises? Yet Jesus Christ, in all His teaching on prayer and forgiveness, again and again, laid down the principle of forgiveness.

There is another angle to unforgiveness. In John Steinbeck's *East of Eden*, one of his characters is a young woman who told her friend, "I threw my stepmother's watch into the canal, and when my father punished me I hated him for weeks — but I finally forgave him."

Her surprised friend: "*You* forgave *him?*"

"Yes," she replied, "I forgave him for punishing me—how was he to know how I felt about my stepmother?"

Has someone done something insufferably selfish to

hurt you? Perhaps there is a reason you don't know anything about. Perhaps the person you despise isn't even aware that you are holding something against him. Have you considered what this is doing to *you*? You are putting yourself into a prison of dislike. *You* are the prisoner.

Several years ago I was asked to be the speaker at a women's week-end retreat. My subject was love and forgiveness. A lady with a distinct southern accent said to me, "I'm so happy! I've been able to forgive my husband's relatives."

A few days later, this same lady introduced me to her husband.

"What did you do to my wife last week-end? She's a different person!"

"It isn't what I did, it's what she did that let God's miracle of love take place." Then turning to his wife, I asked, "What did happen to you?"

Rather self-consciously, she looked up at her husband a moment and then said. "Oh, I learned to love my husband's relatives! I don't know why it's so hard for us Southerners to love our relatives! Anyway, I learned to pray and to forgive. I learned that God loves them as much as He loves me."

"You certainly learned something," commented her husband. "I never saw such a change in anyone!"

Up to this time, this lady, a good church member, had never been bothered by the fact that she couldn't stand her husband's relatives. Face to face with the Saviour, in one of the small prayer groups, she found herself unable to pray, for she herself had need of forgiveness for despising them in her heart. Not for anything they had done, but for just *being* as they were. When she did this, the joy for forgiveness became the joy of new life in Christ flooding her heart, and it was the first thing her husband noticed.

The principle of forgiveness demands a softening of the heart toward a certain person, or the heart becomes like brass, unable to accept God's forgiveness. The way of forgiving others is a way to the Door of Life, where Jesus admits you to the Father's home. The operation of faith and belief in Christ is contingent upon my willingness. This is a powerful door-opener. The door of forgiveness — even if it is not your fault — take it. It will lead you to Christ and to Life.

The one who would possess a forgiving heart must be willing to receive a forgiven heart.

"I believe in the forgiveness of sins." We say it each time we repeat the *Apostles' Creed* in church.

> *Blessed and happy and to be envied are those whose iniquities are forgiven and whose sins are covered up and completely buried. Blessed and happy and to be envied is the person of whose sin the Lord will take no account nor reckon it against him* (Romans 4:7, 8, *Amplified*).

Blessed and happy and to be envied is the person who not only has received a forgiven heart, but who is given the power to forgive those who have sinned against him! This is the power received by those who have become the sons of God. Blessed and happy is the state of that man or woman who is no longer in an unforgiven state, but who is in the enviable state of having his sins forgiven. How far are one's sins removed? Where they shall never be found again: in the depths of the sea! (Micah 7:19). As far as the East is from the West! (Psalm 103:12). In other words, God will never count them against us. Having forgiven us, God forgets completely.

Such love marks a greatness of spirit which belongs to God alone. "Father, forgive them, for they know not what they do," was Jesus' cry from the cross, the symbol forever of the spirit and cost of forgiveness (Luke 23:34, *Amplified*). By such drastic means has the door to forgiveness been opened to us. Having given to us the gift of forgiveness, Christ now calls on us to forgive one another. He has not called us to tread on untried ground. He has not asked us to go where He has not gone. With one difference: He was without sin — He is the One sinned against — and in the last analysis, He is the Forgiving One, and the Forgiver.

> *This is My instruction, that you love one another as I have loved you* (John 15:12, *Berkeley*).

For Discussion

1. Mark 2:5-12. What is the difference between God's forgiveness for us, and ours for each other?
2. Luke 7:47-50. The need for forgiveness; the results.
3. James 5:15, 16. Mark 10:13-16. Share or discuss the power of prayer and "laying on of hands" for release from bitterness, resentment and unforgiveness.

Prayer Time

Silently Read Ephesians 4:32, 5:1, 2 (*Phillips*) and pray for the other party, and for yourself. *God loves you as much as He does me.* Pray this prayer 100 times daily if necessary.

Audibly. Do this, in freedom and with faith: Ask another to lay hands upon you for healing, according to James 5:16 and Mark 10:13-16. The "situation" need not be retold. Memories can be healed, sins forgiven, and wholeness of body, mind and spirit will be yours.

You will, with thanksgiving, be able to love God, to love and to accept yourself, and others. Your open heart will be continually filled with thanksgiving. Philippians 4:6, 7.

9

The Blocked-Off Heart: a sophisticated woman

HUMAN HEARTS are blocked-off from God for many reasons. The outward barriers may look formidable, but they are more easily removed than the inner heart-barriers. Perhaps the reason for this is because we are encouraged as we tackle the outer ones and watch them begin to crumble. But the inner blockades! The prejudices carried from childhood, the hurts or injuries inflicted, the premature bereavements, the loss of usefulness. Why did God let these happen? Or it may be that a person is an existentialist with an excessively practical turn of mind, or without belief in the supernatural, or with a seeming inability to accept the fact of a personal God.

A month ago I knew two women whose inner blockades could be largely defined by that last clause: seemingly unable, or at least, unwilling to believe that God is a Person who loves them in a personal way. Today, one of them has already let the walls crumble, and has found faith in a personal God. The other — a lovable woman in her early sixties — still seems unable or unwilling, but our hearts are high with hope, since the conversion of her friend. What is not possible with man, is possible with God. There is nothing impossible with God! (Matthew 19:26).

It would not be factual to say that A.P., aged 59, had believed in nothing all the years of her full and interesting life, even though her heart had been strangely blocked-off from God. She had always been a woman of faith in a power higher than human power.

"I believed in a Force," she explained, "a great all-powerful Force somewhere in the universe, and I also believe in some kind of life after death. But in spite of a Christian childhood, I was never able to center my faith in a personal God. Somehow I felt I was belittling God to attempt to think of Him as being one with Jesus Christ."

A.P.'s life had been a truly sophisticated one — so authentically so, in fact, that she would be embarrassed at the thought. She is as familiar with Europe as America, helped reclaim and rebuild an island in the Bahamas, for many years owned one of the real show-places among the magnificent ranches in Arizona, and until recently, was a woman of reasonable wealth. For the past several years, she held a responsible position with a leading business firm, and owns her own home and apartment building on the near north side of Chicago.

It is never easy to watch the circumstances of one's life begin to crumble; it is still more difficult at 59 years of age. One loss followed another and none were solely her fault.

For fourteen years, one of her closest friends had been a follower of Jesus Christ, and in her heart she knew fourteen years was a long enough time to have tried something and found it to be true. Her friend's life had been totally changed, although immediately following her friend's conversion, A.P. had been turned almost into an atheist (as she expresses it) because that friend was so dogmatic about her new life! However, the friend matured in Christ with the years, and when the losses began to fall, their friendship had been renewed and deepened.

One night at dinner, early in the spring of 1963, A.P. said, "The time has come for me, what are you waiting for? When you were first converted you almost flattened me with your stupid talk! Now what do I have to do — hit you over the head to get you to tell me the next step? Can't you see I've got to find God the way you did? Help me to Him — tonight!"

The two friends hurried to the Christian's home nearby, and without removing her coat, A.P. said, "I try to pray at home. I *try* so hard to make the contact you talk about, but I can't do it. He doesn't hear me. He isn't there — as a Person for me. I can't believe what you believe about Jesus Christ. I'm blocked somehow — I can't believe He's one with God."

Her friend made one simple suggestion: "Have you tried speaking directly to Jesus Christ when you pray?"

A.P. was tense, and suddenly childlike. "No, is that what I have to do? Will that make Him real to me?"

The moments that followed were deep with the Presence of the Living God. A.P.'s friend led her simply into conversation with Jesus.

"Ask Him to forgive you for every sin you've ever committed, consciously or unconsciously." A.P. did.

"Now tell Him you want to give yourself to Him." She did this, too, and the tears streamed down her face, with the tears, the tension lines began to fade away.

"Now," her friend continued, "thank Him for loving you."

The Christian friend's prompting was no longer needed. A.P. thanked Him for loving her, but after that she "took off" on her own and began to talk to Him with the first certainty of her life. Hers was a wide-open heart now, and her response as sure and free as a child.

"Thank You for loving me, and oh, *thank You for being available!* Thank You, Thank You, for being so available to me!"

Her gratitude poured out to Him in these simple words, but her changed life since that spring night shows her gratitude even more startlingly. A.P. now has patience where impatience had been a characteristic. She has love, where before there was marked disdain. Her fears and tensions are thinning out as she learns how to be her real, relaxed self for the first time in her life. At almost sixty, she is younger than she has been since childhood.

Her christian friend told me over and over, "It was as though a block had been removed instantly! As soon as she spoke directly to Jesus Christ as the God whom she longed for, the block was gone."

This is the dynamic simplicity of the Gospel of God. He planned it this way. He came for this reason in the Person of His Son, Jesus Christ, so that the vague, troublesome block between His own heart and ours, could be removed once and for all.

A.P.'s problems have not changed, but *she* has been changed in the midst of them. She is no longer trying to exert her inherent will power to hold her poise, or to contain her temper. She is clearly now *a child of God*, with a child's open heart toward Him. Her child's heart has no barrier, no block to work its way around. The way is clear. The door is open. She has direct, simple, constant access to the One whom she has discovered *to be the Door*.

Whatever the seeming cause of your blocked-off heart, speaking directly to the One who called Himself the Door, will remove the block forever. He is always reaching toward you. Once your heart makes a responsive contact with God in Jesus Christ, the block is gone.

Thomas asked,

> *Lord . . . how can we know the way?*

Jesus said,

> *I am the Way and the Truth and the Life; no one comes to the Father except by (through) Me. If you had known me — had learned to recognize Me — you would also have known My Father. From now on you know Him, and have seen Him.*

Philip said to Him:

Lord, show us the Father — cause us to see the Father, that is all we ask; then we shall be satisfied.

Jesus replied,

Have I been with all of you for so long a time and do you not recognize and know Me yet? Philip? Any one who has seen Me has seen the Father (John 14:5-9, Amplified).

For Discussion

1. What is the "block" which kept this person from praying?
2. How would you have handled this, or any other intellectual block?
3. Underline the answer her friend gave her.
4. This is an example of over-simplification. When can it best be used?

Prayer Time

Silently What "blocks" are in your own mind? Name them. Are you aware of "blocks" in others? Pray for them.

Audibly Suggestion: Let your group break into twos; admit your blocks to one another and to Jesus (who is present). Speak directly to him, as A.P. did, and give thanks.

10

Disillusioned: he'd been saved nineteen times

> *Come to Me all you who labor and are heavily burdened and I will rest you. Take My yoke on you and learn of Me, for I am gentle and humble of heart, and you will find rest for your souls; for My yoke is easy and My burden is light* (Matthew 11:28, 29, 30, *Berkeley*).

"I'VE BECOME A CHRISTIAN nineteen different times and I'm not sure I'm a Christian right now," said an intelligent, personable man in his late thirties. "I don't see any evidence of God's Person or Personality within me."

On several different occasions I've listened understandingly to S.F. I can understand his thoughts, ideas and experiences as he interprets them because I sensed his religious background. It was the same as mine.

Not that I can give him any acceptable answers, for he knows them all before he asks! A person like S.F. has to discover his own answers. Understanding is the most valuable thing I can give him as another human being — understanding, and the freedom to find his own way at his own pacing. I could share what I've found, but right now, he's not interested in me, he's interested in himself, and why he is like he is, and who or what is to blame.

He smiled when I asked him if he had any particular goal in mind. He knows as well as I, that any spiritual goal he may single out, will immediately be under fire from another part of his agile mind. He defeats himself at every turn, dissects himself, turns himself inside out, in such a correct analysis that he doesn't leave himself a single leg to stand on. Such is the complexity of human nature which seems to thrive better with only one eye open.

Complex as it may be, human nature has an adaptive gadget too. It is so constituted that if a ray of light comes through on any one important subject, it seems to spread out and encompass other trouble areas also. Thus hope and balance will be restored even when there are myriads of questions still unanswered.

There is a proper blending between what you can do and what God can do in the matter of carrying life's burdens. Life tends to put a heavy hand on the scale making an improper balance, putting all the weight and burden on us. God never actually intended it to be there at all. Jesus Christ came to lift our burdens, to take the weight of sin, failure and guilt — not to increase them! He never intended for us to carry our own burdens. He carried them for us, once and for all, on the cross. This is the Good News in a nutshell: *It is finished*: *your sins are forgiven — Come to Me . . . you will find rest.*

S.F. has more than one set of problems existent in that first statement. There is the problem of always getting started and never arriving. Always *becoming* and never *being* a Christian. Always planting and never sprouting.

Then there is the big question: Doesn't he realize God loves him just as he is? What does he mean, no evidence within? God's love is not like man's — singling out deserving persons on which to bestow favors, or withholding favors from undeserving persons. If S.F. knew this one fact, really *knew* it (God loves him) he couldn't make that statement in the first paragraph.

After "trying" nineteen times, S.F. may think he knows a great deal about Jesus Christ. What he doesn't know is that he's really in the dark about Christ. How do I know? He wouldn't be making a statement like that in the present tense if he wasn't in the dark. All he can see at present are the violent contradictions in Life. In this whole world of people, his loneliness is unbearable for his problems are unique (to him). There is no one else (he thinks) who runs into as many contradictions and up so many blind alleys!

Yes, S.F. knows about Christians and Christian doctrines and practices. After all "nineteen times" covers a few years, remember. But just how much can one find out about God's love from God's people?

One *should* be able to know God's love from knowing Christians, argues some hungry-hearted man searching for the Living Bread which he knows nourishes and sustains him. It's true, one should. But how much can a person know about marriage just because he knows married people? And if his marriage fails, can he justly blame that failure on the institution of marriage? Obviously, repetition is not the secret of success in marriage, either.

In physical birth it takes nine months for the fetus to become a human being. Who knows how long it takes for a spiritual birth? Nine days or nine years? Yet the result of birth is the same: a new kind of existence for a new kind of being. This is true of both physical and spiritual birth. Each person is different, and responds differently, as God's Spirit moves in our inner hearts — to get our attention, to bring us to spiritual birth. We become Christians when we respond to Christ. But to be forever becoming and never to start being is tragic.

The little seed dies in the earth in order to send up a sprout and become a living plant. It is no longer a seed. Each man and woman dies to himself and to herself, in a way, when they respond to Christ and say, "Lord, I believe. Take me, I accept you."

Now, considering the illustrations of marriage, birth

and the seedling, what kind of sense does it make for someone to keep doing the same thing over and over? Getting married over and over. Getting born over and over. Planting, sprouting, pulling it up, and repeating the process over and over.

Speaking of the eternal quality of spiritual birth as contrasted to the short-lived quality of physical birth, Peter writes,

> *For you have been born again, not from a perishable, but from an imperishable sperm through the living and lasting message of God; for, "All flesh is as grass . . . withers and . . . drops off, but the Word of the Lord endures forever." And this is the message that has been preached to you* (I Pet. 1:23-25, *Berkeley*).

Being a Christian is something like getting married. It's by far the best illustration I've found. The courtship is the *becoming* period which ends in *being married*. The process goes like this: We become acquainted, we become aware of each other's differing personality traits, we become accustomed to each other's presence. We begin to make plans, permanent plans — to become engaged, to get married. This is the *becoming* time which necessarily precedes the *being* time. A man cannot be a husband until he becomes a bridegroom. A woman cannot be a wife until she becomes a bride. The preparation time is over, they are pronounced man and wife. They are married. Now they can start *being* husband and wife.

This all may sound like a mere play on words, but there is more than meets the eye for the person who really wants to know. When did the marriage really begin? When the minister pronounced them man and wife? Well, you say that was the legal beginning. Is there another beginning? "I was married to Jane in my heart weeks before I asked her," admitted a young husband. "We were one in spirit long before the legal ceremony," said a man and wife. This isn't always true, because human beings are human beings; sometimes it is years before a man and woman learn to love each other and become joined in heart and spirit.

When does a person become a Christian? There is no set rule. It depends upon the individual and what goes on in his heart as he responds to Jesus Christ. But the *becoming* does take place in the spirit, then the being shines through into the life, and people say, "He's a Christian."

Becoming is when something happens, as a caterpillar becomes a butterfly, or a Miss becomes a Mrs. Becoming speaks of undergoing change or development. Being is the end of becoming.

I understand that both marriage and birth have their limitations as illustrations when it comes to the true meaning of being a Christian. But as far as they go, a great deal of light can be thrown on the subject. We only can understand some spiritual truths in the light of the natural things which God has provided by way of illustration.

There is another analogy about being married and being a Christian that has helped me. The legal transaction of marriage is a *constant*, like a straight line, drawn "until death do us part." Or, like an ideal, and without ideals we are all lost! That straight line represents the status quo — our *relationship* is that of marriage. But there is another line to be drawn under that one which represents the everyday working out of that relationship. This line has its ups and downs, its quiet plateaus and its stormy ridges. This *variable* line is our actual *fellowship*, based on our dispositions, the weather, finances, the children and a host of other conditional things. In marriage, where two people are adapting to each other, it is the set of the mind, the will to love and to be loved, the resistance to escape or flight, the discipline of being bound to one another for better or for worse.

In the Christian life it is much the same. Our *relationship* with Christ is finished. He did it all. Relationship is the constant, it is not dependent on what you or I do. He forgave our sins. He finished the sin question, reconciling all mankind to God. Is He ever going to change?

Our relationship is a constant; our fellowship is the variable. For *fellowship* depends on us, on how we follow through in our love, obedience and discipleship. We go up and down, but thank God — we are as it were — married to Christ in a constant relationship. He holds us, knowing that the "downs" can produce more character, provide fresh cleansing, new humility, and that the "ups" can encourage us, give us joy, and help us to fulfill our calling to be His. Therefore, instead of being victims of discouragement, we are continually encouraged, knowing we are loved and accepted "for better or for worse."

Not being able for certain reasons to follow through on my conversation with S.F., I'm limited to thinking through the various reasons which might have contributed to his predicament.

First, we would want to know about his conversion and what assurance he has to rest his faith upon. Second, we would try to find the real reason for his discouragement: which could be lack of Biblical teaching, or knowledge of how to handle sin and failure. Third, it could be lack of knowledge of deeper Christian truth and what true maturity is. All three are important, and each one suggests other possibilities which could be explored if necessary.

First, regarding conversion. What kind of evidence is he looking for? Do others see Christ in him? Does he know the difference between trusting in Christ and in his own efforts?

"I want the kind of a conversion experience," writes a desperate woman who has been searching for years, "that my brother has. He's filled with joy and bubbling over all the time. I want to know I'm really saved." It may be that her brother has a totally different disposition from hers. God's life comes through us according to our natural dispositions. This woman is looking at herself. She needs to look away from self, from her brother, from her own ideas of any experience or its results, and look into the face of Jesus Christ. She needs to direct her attention to Him, to His Person, rather than a personal experience—that will come.

Remember, the Gift comes with the Giver. But which is more important? If she will put her attention upon Him, He will bring the change within and without. When the branch continues to grow in and on the vine, fruit-bearing is inevitable, said Jesus in His discourse in the 15th chapter of John.

Many good people are discouraged in their long struggle to become God's children, because they do not understand the difference between relationship and fellowship. You wouldn't believe the hundreds of people doubting their salvation, and questioning God's power to save them, unless you'd see the mail that comes to the desks of people who write books like this. They're trying to believe in an experience, wanting a feeling, seeking for assurance.

In my book, *Prayer — Conversing With God*, there is a chapter titled, "Prayer Begins a New Relationship," in which I tell the story of Grace, an intelligent university student, and her struggle to believe that *she* could become a Christian. It was not until she began to follow through on the sequence of the verbs found in John 10:27 that the truth broke through! "My sheep hear my voice, and I know them, and they follow me: And I give unto them eternal life. . . ." First they hear, then they follow, then He gives them eternal life. Question: when did they become His sheep? Before or after Jesus gave them eternal life? He calls them His sheep before they heard or received the gift. The first step is to hear and to begin to follow the Shepherd, then He does all the giving.

Because He is the all-knowing God, He knows the heart is responding, is going to respond, will continue to respond. When do we become His sheep? When do we become Christians? I think, in one sense, we'll have to wait and ask Him some day! In another sense, we can know, just as we know when we got married, because we said *yes*. To those who never had a definite transaction — well, that's all right. I have a friend who doesn't know the date on which she was born because her parents are both dead and neglected to record her birth. But she's alive, so she picked her own birthday! Living people aren't the discouraged ones. It's the half-alive, overly-conscientious ones, who need more teaching in the Scriptures, who succumb to doubt and discouragement — tools of the evil one.

Second, the real reason for his discouragement. Before I even consider failure in discipleship and maturity, I'd like to make sure the person knows something about the true nature of God and of Christ's finished work on the cross. Along with this comes the necessity to understand something of one's own nature.

The true nature of God, that He loves us, knows all about us and accepts us, has already been discussed in other chapters, but I cannot emphasize too strongly the need for repetition of this basic truth.

Let's consider that discouragement can be due to a lack of understanding regarding the truth of our relationship with God. The cross of Christ can make that relationship a *constant* instead of a variable. If there were only the latter, we'd all be sunk!

After my own conversion at fifteen years of age, I had the ever-present problem of deciding between right and wrong. And what happens to one's Christianity in the struggle? I saw some of my friends slipping back into old ways, getting "saved" over and over. Each time it seemed easier for them to "slip away" and harder for them to "get through" again. I'll admit to a little "slipping" myself; but — due to what guardian angel I'll never know — I told no one. I kept it to myself, took it to the Lord Jesus, received His forgiveness and went right on (I John 1:9).

It was at least ten years later, after I'd been struggling with failure in my life, and how incompatible it was, that the truth finally dawned upon me. The secret of the Christian life is not in my sinless life, but in Christ's sinless life!

I began to learn two things. What to do with failure, and how to read the Scriptures aright, regarding God's nature and the meaning of the cross. We'll get into the subject of failures in Chapter 17, but what I began to learn about the atonement (at-one-ment) of Christ put my mind so completely at rest that He could then teach me regarding His truth.

I had sought my first answers to sin and failure in an experience which in theory promised perfection in love, but in practice demanded perfection in conduct. It was so impossible that I despaired of ever pleasing God. If pleasing God demands perfection of any kind, how could I ever be accepted by God as His child?

I found the answer in two things: First, it all depends on how you define sin. Second, it all depends on how completely Christ took care of sin on that cross.

When sin was defined as any *known* transgression of the law, it threw me into the dilemma of when is sin, sin? When is it a mistake of judgment? When is my carnal nature to blame? And when is it just human nature? I deliberateliy avoided making choices, so I would not be considered responsible and culpable.

When sin is defined as any lack or want of conformity to the law of God — that takes in everything — whether I choose or refuse to choose, no matter which of my natures is involved, I am responsible, to know and to decide (on the spot or afterwards) whether I am following God's ways or going my own way. Which in fact is the essence of all sin, on either side of the scale.

Another revelation came to me, which enabled me to accept the "eight ball" which that last definition handed me. I hope you're following me, for while it isn't easy to put this into black and white, it is glorious to try, because it marked the beginning of a new era of rest, relaxation, trust and love for me. I was beginning to understand what it meant to live in the Spirit.

The answer to my continual guilt I found in the ninth chapter of Hebrews, verses 25-28. I'm also forever indebted to the friend who asked me a couple of questions.

"How many times did Christ have to die?"

There was only one answer, "Only once."

"How many of your sins did He take care of then?"

There was only one answer, "All of them."

"Past? Present?" and before he finished with "Future?" I saw the point, and I've seen it ever since, again and again in the Scriptures until I wonder how blind I was, never to have seen it before!

If Christ did not completely take the sins of the whole world upon Himself at Calvary, what then? If He did not take all my sins . . . past, present and future . . . upon Himself, then does He have to come and die again? If He did not do a complete and finished work of saving us all by giving Himself, what then? The truth is, He did it once and for all! For all time, and for all men! He had no intention of offering Himself regularly (as the Old Testament sacrifices were offered). He came as The Lamb of God to take away the sin of the world (John 1:29), once and for all!

What does this mean for me, for you? Why, it's like money in the bank, deposited to my name, waiting there until I sign my name on the check and draw upon it. It's better than that, because being "in Christ" and having Christ "in me" is a living relationship, that issues in a day-by-day fellowship. He takes care of everything.

That's why I can confidently say now, "I'm saved," in three tenses, three dimensions. I have been saved, I am being saved, and I shall be saved. What happened to me at fifteen years of age is going on now, daily, and shall continue in this life and in the life hereafter, because I am a Son, a child, in the Father's House.

I don't have to continue to skip over certain Bible verses. I don't have to be on one side of the theological fence or the other, and I don't have to sit on the fence either. All the truth in Jesus Christ is mine, and what I don't understand intellectually, I do understand emotionally, because love will wait for further enlightenment. I'm learning more every day about Jesus Christ and His love for me, and for all mankind.

Discouraged? Discouraged when I'm loved by God who has become my eternal Saviour, who has not only taken care of sins I've already committed, but who has already taken care of those I've not yet committed! No, discouragement is for those who have no hope of a Saviour, those who have never heard, or those who don't know.

Joy is born of hope. Hope is offered to all. Faith is waiting for all. All who will respond to the invitation,

> *Come unto me, all ye that labour and are heavy laden, and I will give you rest* (Matthew 11:28).

For Discussion

1. Name several reasons, or possible situations, which could have contributed to the state in which S.F. found himself? (such as: others? himself? theology? unrealized ideals? recurring failure? etc.)
2. What illustrations does the author give to help us make subjective truth more objective? Which is most helpful to you?
3. What is one of the great secrets of living a Christian life?

Prayer Time

Silently Read, in your Bible, the scriptures used in this chapter. Face the reason for your own discouragement.

Audibly Pray for one another, by name, with love and understanding and thanksgiving.

11

Rejected: the search for happiness

> *"If you knew what God can give . . . and if you knew who it is that said to you, 'Give me a drink,' I think you would have asked him, and he would have given you living water!" . . . "Everyone who drinks this water will be thirsty again. But whosoever drinks the water I will give him will never be thirsty again. For my gift will become a spring in the man himself, welling up into eternal life"* John 4:10, 13, 14, *Phillips*).

"I'VE HAD AN UNQUENCHABLE heart-thirst all my life. I guess that's why everything went to pieces — but maybe it had to, or I'd never know God's love."

The first time I saw Nancy H., whose honest statement you've just read, she was standing beside her husband Dick, on the platform of the Pocono *Faith At Work* Conference. They were telling us the story of their lives.

Nancy continued, "We've been married a year and a half and we have four children." The audience gasped audibly.

"Honey," said Dick, "tell them the truth, and why you married me in the first place."

"We've been married and divorced and re-married," she explained, "and this year and a half things are really different because Christ is first in our hearts. I married Dick for two reasons: First, because I needed a *father*; and second, because his family had more *money* than our family!"

"And I married you," Dick continued with his part of the story, "because I needed a *mother*, and I thought I was in love with you when I was only in love with myself. When the children began to come (and we have four), they really had no mother or father because we didn't know how to be parents. We failed each other, we failed ourselves, and worst of all, we failed our children. I started to 'step out,' separation came next. Divorce was inevitable."

Friends from the Winnetka First Presbyterian Church found Nancy (and not "playing God" by trying to mend the marriage) loved her and included her as a person. She gave her heart to Christ, began to find her real self and to pray for Dick.

One morning, quite unexpectedly, he called for the children and walked into church with them, fully knowing his need. Because the Christians took him in and *loved him*, he was able to accept their forgiveness, then God's forgiveness, and finally to forgive himself.

"It makes a difference when your ultimate dependence is in Christ," said Nancy in a recent telephone conversation. "Once we stopped depending on each other, and began to depend on God's love, we were able to really love one another. Human love is so conditional — on what *you* have for dinner to how *you* raise the children! But when you love God first, then you become a channel of God's love for your mate."

There is a door to human fulfillment.

There is a door to human happiness.

But it's not always what you think it is. Your searching heart may be ever so responsive, but without the Shepherd, who leads you to the Door, it may take the wrong way. The Shepherd is everywhere seeking for Responsive Hearts, but some of us are so busy responding in other directions that we aren't even aware that He is reaching toward us. His love is a waiting love, a watching love. He is watching your varied excursions here and there, as you are searching, knocking, always looking for the desire of your heart.

We make our own little cisterns, hoping the rain will fall and fill them up so we can drink and drink and be satisfied. We make our own little bread-sticks and eat and eat, trying to believe that we've found the answer, the reason for existence. Then someone steps on our cistern and breaks it — it can no longer hold water; our bread-sticks run out, and we find ourselves both hungry and thirsty.

There is in the heart of every person a dissatisfaction and longing which never seems to come to fulfillment. This is eventually true of those who have, as well as those who have not. In the midst of every seemingly complete situation, or soon afterward, there is a well of loneliness which never seems to find completion.

Jesus Christ was aware of this.

> "*If you knew what God can give . . . you would have asked . . . and He would have given you. . . .*" "*Everyone who drinks this water will be thirsty again*" (John 4:10, 13, *Phillips*).

Are you thirsty? Are you hungry? Have you been rejected? Are you searching for someone to understand you? Will "earth-water" satisfy you?

Jesus promises a drink of water that will turn into a bubbling well-spring within us to last for eternity. This is His own Spirit within us, which is given to us as a gift, when we ask for it. Drink of this water and you will never be thirsty.

Why does it take so long to hear the Shepherd's voice? Why are we so deaf and dumb and blind where He is concerned? Why does there have to be so much uncertainty and confusion? Perhaps the answer lies in the fact that only the sick need a physician, not the well. This is one of our Lord's own answers to His coming into the world (Mark 2:17).

The intensity of your search will depend on how hungry and thirsty you are. Without a sense of need, we each continue to go our way . . . apart from God, away from God. Sometimes our sense of need is so apparent we throw caution to the wind, and openly ask, seek and knock. Sometimes our need is so secretly desperate that we suffer silently, looking in vain for one single person who will understand.

Because our hearts were made for love, finding the right person to belong to is the ultimate goal of life to half the persons alive right now. Radio, TV, novels and magazines are filled with stories of people who are searching for someone to love them. I heard an old ditty on the radio the other day, and instantly recognized it as the one of the false-doors-of-promise to lure us on:

> I wanta go where you go,
> Do what you do,
> Sigh when you sigh,
> Love when you love,
> Then . . . I'll be happy!

Is this happiness? To be with, go with, laugh and sigh with, love and be loved? To spend every possible moment day and night with another human being in your presence or at the end of a telephone line? Does this add up to happiness? The kind of happiness you long for?

Yes, yes! Say those who are still looking.

Yes, yes! Say those who have just found.

No, no! Say those who have just lost, and keep looking.

No, a thousand times no, say those who have been thoroughly disillusioned half-a-dozen times, and keep longing.

But longing for what and for whom? Longing for lost happiness, looking for a new love? Defeated by the past and scheming for the future? Blaming God, life and everyone but yourself — does this sound familiar?

Maybe it isn't some*one* to understand you, maybe it's a career, financial success, driving ambition to take you to the top in your field. Newspapers are full of stories of people who've knocked on all these doors, and yet — apparently life wasn't worth living.

At which door are you knocking? Have you recognized the true character of your own heart? As you read this chapter, or any other chapter which you may have selected, have you recognized your own Searching Heart? Whatever is blocking you off, causing you to rebel, or to suffer, if you will look again you'll find that there is a heart within you to turn to the Lord who loves you. Where there is a bit of willingness, let it grow into more willingness. Where there is some openness, let it grow into more openness.

> *"Ask and it will be given to you.*
> *Search and you will find.*
> *Knock and the door will be opened for you.*
> *The one who asks will always receive; the one who is searching will always find, and the door is opened to the man who knocks. If any of you were asked by his son for bread would you be likely to give him a stone, or if he asks for a fish would you give him a snake? If you then, for all your evil, quite naturally give good things to your children, how much more likely is it that your Heavenly Father will give good things to those who ask Him?"* (Matthew 7:7-11, *Phillips*).

If your answer doesn't come right away, wait. In my experience, I've found God needs time to change me before He can give me what He knows I need. If I'm asking for what I think is bread, and He knows it will destroy me like a serpent, He withholds it. In His great love, He changes my very desires so He is able to give me what He knows I need. Isn't it wonderful to know God is like this?

> When your answer comes, it will be *bread.* Jesus said, *I am the Bread of life. He who comes to Me will never hunger and he who believes in Me shall not suffer thirst any more* (John 6:35, *Berkeley*).

We need love, but human love is only adequate and balanced when God's love is present. Then there can be meaning in every other part of life. When human relationships are off-balance, and we are unsure of our acceptance by God, there is an emptiness which all the wells of un-named waters cannot fill.

"To be whole persons," said Nancy and Dick, "we need love both on a horizontal *and* a vertical plane, then we can give to one another what God is giving to us."

To be a whole person means to belong. God made us with a built-in capacity not only *to belong* but *to possess;* these capacities are the warp and woof of human fabric. When we use them to bind one another, we are knocking at the door of broken promises. When we let ourselves respond, and be possessed by the Good Shepherd we become free to find ourselves, because we are found! We become a being, a person. We belong as a child, as a son in the family of God, accepted and forgiven and loved. We belong to Him, He belongs to us, and we belong to each other.

Jesus knew the meaning of rejection, but He also knew He was accepted by His Father.

This is what the Father says of Him:

> *This is my beloved Son: hear him* (Mark 9:7, KJV).
>
> *Thou art My Son, My Beloved; in Thee I am delighted* (Mark 1:11, *Berkeley*).

This is what Jesus says of His relationship with the Father.

> . . . *I do nothing of My own accord, but tell things just as the Father has taught Me. My Sender is with Me: He does not leave Me alone, for I do invariably what pleases Him* (John 8:28, 29, *Berkeley*).

This is what John says of Christ's relationship with men:

> *He was in the world and the world came into being through Him, yet the world did not know Him. He came to His own and His own did not receive Him. But to those who did receive Him,*

He granted ability to become God's children, that is, to those who believe in His name; who owe their birth neither to human blood, nor to physical urge, nor to human design, but to God (John 1:10-13, *Berkeley*).

Loved ones, we are God's children now, and what we shall be has not yet been shown; but we know that when He has been revealed we shall resemble Him, for we shall see Him as He is (I John 3:2, *Berkeley*).

When does one receive eternal life, or the son-relationship? When he comes to Jesus Christ. When he feels that hunger in his heart. When he begins to respond to Jesus Christ, as the God who can forgive his sins and make him a son in the Father's house.

For Discussion

1. With the pressures of life, personal relationships, and responsibilities . . . what is the answer to the constant gnawing within? The hunger for acceptance and for understanding?
2. Those doubts, hungers, questions buried within a man, can they ever be fully shared? Can one human ever find this inner fulfillment with another human?
3. Or . . . is one confusing God with humans, and expecting people to respond as only God can? Can the hunger of the heart be fed by any other food than the never-changing love of God?

Prayer Time

Silently Meditate on the Scriptures in italics. Could the answer be: that, having been fed with the Bread from Heaven, each of us must share with another, what we have been given, and what they are able to receive?

Audibly Express your gratitude, and affirm your openness of heart for a fresh supply.

12

The Responsive Heart: could be yours

ANYONE CAN HAVE a responsive heart.

A responding heart is an answering heart, for response implies answering, reply, reaction. Just as the physical ear is so constructed that it picks up both welcome and unwelcome sounds from the outer world, so the inner ear of the heart is sensitive to wave lengths from the spiritual world.

There are three things implied here. First, the source of the stimulation. Second, the receptor, upon whom the stimulation acts. And lastly, the purpose of this interaction.

Who can be a Christian? Anyone who is responding to Jesus Christ. "A Christian," writes P. Carnegie Simpson (*The Fact of Christ*), "is anyone who is responding to whatever meanings of Christ are, through God's Spirit, being brought home to his intellectual or moral conscience. This is a definition at once exhaustive of the profoundest Christianity and admissive of the simplest."

This being true, response is not like an electric light switch that can be turned on and off at will. Response is the vibrating power of the electricity itself, being generated at the dynamo, seeking an outlet for its energy and power. Shall we say, our ability and decision *to choose* can be likened to the light switch, for the response is already at work within us, ready to be released, to be acknowledged, to be harnessed, to be transformed into action, overt action.

Response is common to all mankind. We can respond in every part of our being: intellectually, emotionally, spiritually and physically. With ingenuity we can perfect circumstances through which our responses may become satisfactorily fulfilled. This is what the whole world is busily doing twenty-four hours a day. The person who is aware of a response in any area immediately seeks a satisfactory outlet.

Let us consider three things implied by response. The first cause, or source of the stimulation, is God Himself. In a recent Florida conference, Dr. Frank Laubach repeated this sentence and I'll never forget it. *God is speaking all the time, all the time, all the time.* Whenever I'm reminded of this truth, I am immediately aware that God *is* speaking — and what am I doing? Being receptive or being preoccupied. It's not that I deliberately turn a deaf ear to God, it's just that I am busy with other things.

I've been a convinced Christian since the age of fifteen. My conversion story is in the chapter on "The Willing Heart." I'm only beginning to find out about the real nature of God. The more I find out and the more I share, the greater God becomes to me. Whatever the problem, however puzzling the situation, remembering what God is like is the solution to comfort and sanity.

Somewhere back in the Garden of Eden man broke his connection and communication with God and went his own way. Ever since, God has been reaching with unutterable love and longing toward His lost ones. Being the eternal omniscient God, He knows everything. Before He created the earth He knew mankind would "get lost" and move away from Him. I've come to see more clearly what David meant in Psalm 19, when he writes that everything in the heavens and the earth are declaring God's character and His purpose toward us. Stop and think about it: The four seasons speak to us of life, death and resurrection; the planetary system, with the great sun around which moves our own universe, deriving all light and life from that sun, speaks to us also. Look where you will, old age, or infancy, nature and all that nature contains (the forces of good and evil), in all these things God is speaking to those who have ears to hear.

In Psalm 139, David declares that God knows all about each person even before birth, and cares about each one. When I sit down or get up, when I walk or when I rest, before I speak the words, He knows everything. Is there anywhere I go where He is not? If I fly like a bird to the ends of the earth, He is there; if I climb to heaven, He is there; if I make my bed in hell, He is there.

God is love. This is His nature. But what is the purpose of His love? The purpose of love is to reach toward the loved one, to make him aware, to supply needs and to give gifts. Love never sits idly in a corner waiting; love is always actively engaged in seeking response from the loved one.

> *See what* [*an incredible*] *quality of love the Father has given (shown, bestowed on) us, that we should* [*be permitted to*] *be named and called and counted the children of God! And so we are!* (I John 3:1, *Amplified*).

God's love is shown in little things as well as big things. The greatest gift He gave to the world was Himself, in the Person of His Son.

> *For God so loved the world, that he gave his only begotten Son, that whosoever believeth in him should not perish, but have everlasting life* (John 3:16, KJV).

To be apart from God is to perish; to come near to Him, to communicate with Him, means life.

Our response is an answer to His advances toward us. He made advances to the Old Testament people (they responded and rebelled). He made advances to those living in New Testament times through the Person of His dear Son, they responded and rebelled. He is making advances to every living person today through His Holy Spirit — and what are we doing? Practically the same thing that our human ancestors did: we respond, or we rebel. Even worse, we are sometimes totally unconscious that He is there, or that His love is reaching through to us.

The purpose of His reaching toward us is that communication might be restored between us, that the broken relationship might be healed. After that, there is full opportunity for cooperation, interaction and sharing in all the purposes of God for us and His world. And on a very personal, heart-to-heart, face-to-face basis, for being a Christian is no deepfreeze relationship. The warm Father-love of God, His constant giving, caring, forgiving, understanding, all-knowing love has been fully shown to us. How? Through Jesus Christ.

Everything about Christ revealed the loving kindness of God — even when some did not respond. In His lifetime on earth He knew the inevitable result of their own rebellion.

Since God has given us Jesus Christ, is there anything He withholds from us? No, having given us His dearest treasure, the whole storehouse is open. Open to whom? To all who will respond, to all with responding hearts. The first response is to His love for you. He loves you. He loves you just as you are: "He cares about you. He forgives you. He is there — yes, there with you now. You are *responding* to Him as you read this, whether you are aware of it or not."

In these chapters, we are reading the actual experiences of people who responded to God, who, by His love, are being drawn to Him. "Every heart can be a responsive heart: the open heart, the willing heart, the thankful heart, the repentant heart; yes, even the rebellious and blocked off hearts are responsive hearts, because night precedes day, and the negative attracts the positive. You can become a Christian, whoever you are."

You are more important than any method. True, you may want to know *how* to find God, how to approach Him, how to pray to Him, how to become His child. After reading this far, you may be wanting to know how to respond to God. How does the heart respond? By answering. Is it that simple? Yes, it is. Why not try it? Respond to God, who is drawing you to Himself this very moment. Response is the heart's business.

If you feel you cannot make the contact alone, ask a friend who already knows Christ; put your pride aside and ask for help. If your friend really knows the love of God and knows God through Christ, you'll look back on that time and know one thing for sure: You, yourself, were more important to that friend than any how-to-do-it method he may have known or used.

I can write like this because early in life I discovered that I was a how-to-do-it person. God help the people I spoke to, but I threw the whole book at them, piled it on, until I wonder that anyone ever got through the material to get a look at the Saviour Himself! I wasn't introducing them to a Person — I was telling them *how*.

I seem to have some kind of built-in mechanism that begins to tick whenever a real life situation confronts me. I'm not so good in discussions of principle or philosophy (how and why things work) until I've first had some actual experience in that particular line. But give me a situation where people are concerned and the old wheels go round and ideas pop. I have to watch this tendency, or I'm telling friends what to do and how to do it! My mother said, that until one knows how to handle his resources, they become liabilities instead of assets.

This is where God's love and wisdom came through to me. I discovered I was depending on the method, the outline, the how, and forgetting the spirit: The Spirit of God who could lead me *and* the spirit of the person concerned. With only one major requirement from us both: *Response.* What a beautiful word! Response!

How does one become a Christian? By responding to the pulling of God's love on your heartstrings. God will teach you more and more about His love, His *drawing* love.

> *Every one whom the Father has given Me will come to Me, and I will certainly not cast out anyone who comes to Me. No one is able to come to Me unless the Father who sent Me draws him . . .* (John 6:37, 44, *Berkeley*).

Step by step God taught me, and brought me to the place of emphasizing the person, instead of the method. I have previously told this story in my book, *You Can Witness With Confidence.*

How to become a Christian? It's a good question, except when one gets happy over outlines and methods. We "outline" people to death by using the same thing over and over and seldom give God a chance to meet anyone where he is. The outline was like a crutch; it made me rigid; it kept me under a strain, it kept me from looking right into the face of Jesus Christ and trusting Him. Yes, one should know all the facts about repentance, confession, commitment and salvation, but there is a time when the *hows* must go into the background to be used as needed, and Christ Himself be brought into the foreground.

One summer I saw the difference between understanding an outline and responding to love. The lady was confused. Yes, she'd gone forward in a large campaign, and the "helper" took her through the Scripture verses on "how to become a Christian." Three times the "helper" went through those verses. Afterward, I asked the lady if she had received help.

"I'm so confused — I couldn't seem to understand what she was telling me." We stepped apart from the crowd into a quiet place for a moment and I gave her the essence of the Gospel: *God loves you. God loves you just as you are.* "How . . . can *He* . . . love *me?* How can He love *me* just as I am?"

Over and over she wanted to hear that message, and I told her over and over. With tears in her eyes she said, "Thank You, Lord Jesus, *for loving me!* Thank You!" She responded simply and she was His.

In this situation, you can easily see that the person is more important than the method. She needed to hear that God loved her. Whatever preparation her heart had been given before she "went forward," one thing is sure. God was drawing her and she was responding. With that preparation, she was able to respond further when she found God loved her, and she was able to be grateful and to give thanks.

Giving thanks is the completion of a transaction: that of receiving a gift. She received the Gift of Jesus Christ, the gift of His love. What it all meant, she would be learning later. For now, that was sufficient.

Persons are more important than methods. However, we must know what God said in the Bible, and be able to use it, for He has given it to us as a guidebook — its pages contain His message to us. But let's remember relationships are more important than doctrines. It's important to know theology, but isn't it more important to have a personal relationship with Him, and call Him Father? It's important that you enter the kingdom of heaven, but isn't it more important to know Jesus Christ, the King, than to know the doctrinal background of salvation? Doctrine is to the Christian what the skeleton is to the body. After we've learned the basics, we must then learn to let love take over. And again, sometimes we must love *before* we've learned the basics.

"Love is as warm as intellect is cold. Let's hold the truth in love, not in giving others the third degree! Let's be simple enough to say to our brother, God loves you! Let's be simple enough to say, I love Jesus — do you?"

Who can become a Christian? I can, and I have, by responding to His invitation. You can, by responding to His invitation. Do you have difficulty believing this means *you*, personally? In the old familiar language: acknowledge you are a sinner, you need forgiveness. Jesus Christ has taken all sin upon Himself on the cross and by the miracle of His resurrection you are free and forgiven, and God's son (I Pet. 2:24, 25).

By seeing and believing on the Son, you yourself become a child of God (John 6:40, 47).

> Respond to the still small Voice within you.
> Respond to the love that is drawing you.
> Respond to the Father who wants to make you a son in His house forever.
> Respond, and accept that wondrous Gift of forgiveness, of eternal life, of Jesus Christ living in you, loving you.
> Who can become a Christian?
> The seeking heart, which is a responding heart.
> The one who suddenly realizes that all he has to do is to respond.

For Discussion

1. Read the Scripture references used in this chapter as a basis for your discussion on *response*.
2. What is the pre-requisite for response? Who initiates it?
3. Re-reading Mr. Simpson's definition early in the chapter, discuss how response can be profound and simple at the same time.

4. Discuss the practical solution of how we may place more importance on the person (inner response) than the method — which may be in current use.

PRAYER TIME

Silently Check your own response, your mental-response, your heart-response — by meditating on the last seven sentences of this chapter.

Audibly In simple, direct sentences of prayer, give thanks or express your honest response.

Part II

HOW DIFFERENT SHOULD A CHRISTIAN BE?

13

What a Christian Is and Is Not

A FEW YEARS AGO I read *The Big Fisherman.* One statement the author made caught my attention. When the amazed crowds questioned Peter again and again about Jesus, he always pointed out one thing: The whole purpose and motive of Jesus was to begin a new race of people, a new Kingdom of Love, a new principle operating within the heart of man.

This freshly worded concept of a Christian accomplished two things for me. It made me glad and grateful that I belonged to His kingdom. It also made me want to tell everyone, so that they too could belong.

What do people around you think about Christianity? Do they know what a real Christian is? Or are they more aware of Christians as a group of people who do or don't do certain things — things that set them apart from other people? Or do they think Christians are people who believe certain things, and who have closed minds on most subjects because of this belief?

It's tragic but true. Too often Christians' lives give validity to these questions and sincere searchers for Truth look away from the Christian faith, attempting to find Truth in some other religion or self-development cult.

In fact, it never occurs to most people that Jesus Christ Himself has something to do directly with being a Christian. Undoubtedly such people gather most of their ideas and impressions from those who profess to be Christians.

The whole idea frightens me. How about you? Do

you want people to be like you? We don't expect members of a family to be alike, nor do we expect to judge a whole family by one of its members. For some reason, people who aren't Christians judge Christianity by what Christians are like, what they can and can't do, what they believe or don't believe.

People fail to consider that impressions Christians make don't always give a true concept of Christianity. Therefore, while it's necessary for us to act in a spirit of love, and to be normal, adjusted, maturing people, this isn't enough. We must know how to engage in simple, direct, sincere conversation about the Christian faith. Visual impressions may be off center. Word concepts can be just as confusing. Therefore, we should endeavor to make our faith as clear as possible, and eliminate confusing impressions as rapidly as we see them. We ourselves must know where the center of our faith is.

First of all, Christianity is Jesus Christ. The person of Jesus Christ — not doctrines about Him, nor beliefs about Him, nor even experiences with Him. Being a Christian means that a new existence is in one's inner being. A new life is there, a new motive, a new being. And that being is the Spirit of Jesus Christ, who Himself has come to live with us.

If Christianity is Jesus Christ, what actually is a Christian? A person isn't a Christian because he was born in a Christian nation. Nor is he a Christian because his parents were Christians. Following rules of outward behavior, conforming in language and actions, going to church, joining the church, being baptized, reading the Bible, praying, giving generously, or obeying the Golden Rule, don't make you a Christian. They may be end results in the lives of those who call themselves Christian. But *doing* isn't the important thing. *Being* is the important thing.

What about believing? Does what you believe make you a Christian? James told us that "the devils also believe, and tremble." That doesn't mean that the devils are Christian. Belief is within one's mind. It is good. It is necessary. It is important. Right and good actions are important. But belief and actions must be linked with Life, Life with a capital L, before they can be transformed into real meaning within the individual. Belief and actions can sometimes be based on desire for social or religious approval or any other strong motivation.

I know a college girl who struggled for a week after going to "special" church meetings. Her problem was whether or not she could accept the "ways" of the Christians and give up her "worldly ways." What would her parents think? What would her friends think? After a week of agony, she reached a decision: she would accept the ways of Christians and become a Christian. Two years later, she came to me in great distress because her Christian life didn't seem to be working. After she told me of the decision she made, I had one question to ask: "Where does Jesus Christ come into the picture?" She hadn't considered Him. She hadn't realized that becoming a Christian was opening her heart and life for Jesus Christ to come in and live within her.

I recall an intelligent college girl who came to one of our Colorado camps for a few days. She had cornered people and talked them out of their arguments because hers were more clever, yet she was still searching. When she told me that no one could answer her questions, I had one question to ask her: "Alice, did anyone ever tell you that being a Christian has a supernatural side to it? Some questions we can answer and think through. However, essentially our emotional needs are our deepest needs and 'answers' won't satisfy them. *One* person will — a supernatural Person, whose name is Jesus Christ. Jesus Christ was God in the flesh, alive and living now by His Spirit in the hearts of those who respond to Him. When our emotional needs are met, we have an inner Guide who helps us wade into and tackle our intellectual and volitional needs."

Jesus didn't say, "I will show you the way of Life." He said, "I am the Life." He didn't say, "I will show you the truth." He said, "I am the Truth." "He who has the Son has Life, and he who has not the Son, has not Life." "I am come to give them Life, and Life more abundantly."

The Life He was speaking about is God's invasion of our human life. This comes as we open our hearts in response to His love. For He has done everything that is to be done.

J. B. Phillips' *When God Became Man* is a book that everyone should read. God is right in this human struggle with us. He never defended Himself; He stood courageously for all that He came to do and to teach; He suffered all the torments of mental and physical rejection; He was crucified by the creatures He created.

This is love. This is redemption. This is the price of forgiveness. This is where sin and evil and suffering and death met their Master. For He arose from His grave, and said, "Lo, I will always be with you. I will come to live in you and with you by my Spirit, and you will never be alone. Open your heart, follow me, learn of me."

What is a Christian? A Christian is one who has opened his heart to the Lord Jesus Christ, and who welcomes His presence as an integral part of his own personality. Being a Christian is giving Jesus Christ the opportunity of living His life within you. Being a Christian is learning to love as He loved, to live as He lived.

A Christian is anyone who is responding to Jesus Christ.

For Discussion

1. Read John 6:28-40. How does one get the bread of God?
2. Discuss the questions in the third paragraph. Move form the general to the specific — from what people think, to what *you* think.
3. What kind of an impression do others make on you? What impression do you make on others? Which is the stronger: A conscious or an unconscious witness? Why?
4. Find the paragraph listing "good things" which people do in trying to become a Christian. Why can't *doing* make one a Christian? Why is *being* more important?

Prayer Time

Silently examine your own life, regarding subjects discussed above.

Audibly, then, in a single sentence, express your thanks, and your desire.

14

Who Can Become a Christian?

MANY PEOPLE THINK that if they believe certain things and conform to certain external standards of conduct they are entitled to call themselves Christian. This is a perversion of the Truth.

A Christian is a person to whom the Life of God has been given as a gift. A Christian is someone to whom the secret plan of God has been fulfilled: the placing of the Life of Jesus Christ into a human heart. A Christian is someone who has by this means been joined to a new race of people: God's sons and daughters, whose hearts and lives operate by the laws of Kingdom Love. These are the indwelt ones. These have received the Spirit of Jesus Christ.

To whom can this gift of Life be given? And how does one know when he has received it? Is it possible for anyone to become a Christian? Doesn't the Bible refer to the chosen ones? What does this mean — that God chooses us, or that we choose Him?

First, the difference between two questions must be clarified. The question of *how* to become a Christian has occupied more printed space and been given more time from the pulpit than the question of *who* can become a Christian. God uses many methods to make Himself known, but I'm constantly amazed at how we limit Jesus Christ by insisting upon one or two ways of coming to Him.

The familiar walk-down invitation at a mass meeting and the person-to-person explanation of the plan of salvation are familiar to almost everyone. People can avoid them easily and they do so for varying reasons — mostly because they're not sure what will happen if they give their lives to Jesus Christ.

But the *how* of becoming a Christian isn't really the important question. The important question is: *Who* can become one?

Do *you* want to become a Christian? If you do, you're the one who *can* become a Christian. For the answer is in your heart already if you will take time to look. You're the important one, and what the Great Creator God is doing in your heart needs personal acknowledgment from you first of all. This may or may not involve an overt action such as going forward in response to an invitation. But certainly it should precede such an action.

Jesus said, "No one is able to come to Me unless the Father who sent Me draws him. . . ." (John 6:44, Berkeley). And, "Every one whom the Father has given Me will come to Me" (John 6:37, Berkeley).

Many persons who are reading this chapter can look back into their lives and see the various ways God drew them to Himself before they confessed Christ openly. The God of Love, the God who died on the cross, is seeking you, reaching for you, drawing you to Himself. Not to a set of rules to live by, not to join a certain denomination. He wants you to come to Him.

I want to tell you a true story about a student I met at a privately owned college which required above-average grades for entrance.

It was noon. We were eating lunch together in the college cafeteria. Since it was my first visit to the campus, I was introduced to Bob, the president of the local Inter-Varsity group, to the secretary, the treasurer and other members.

"See that blond guy down at the end of the table? The one eating an apple? That's Tom. He's our publicity chairman. He makes all the posters. He's an art major."

Someone got Tom's attention and we waved at each other from opposite ends of the table. Then under his breath Bob volunteered this information: "But you know, Ros, we aren't sure that Tom's a Christian."

"How's that?" I asked. "Hasn't anyone talked with him to find out?"

"Well, you know how it is. It's kind of a personal matter and we — well, we —"

I hastened to assure him that I understood. I understood too well. It's so easy to talk about anything and everything except what the heart believes.

Too many times a young person's beliefs about God and Jesus Christ are the result of all the things he has heard during the growing-up process. Such thoughts are scarcely beliefs. They're seed-ideas belonging to grownup people which were planted in his heart as a child, but they have grown into a jumble which bears little or no fruit.

Too many times there's no one to help you reassemble things — your ideas about God and yourself, past, present and future — so you can know what you do believe.

Then again, a person may be forced to declare himself as believing in Jesus Christ, just because of pressure from others, when he really doesn't know what it's all about.

To get back to my "informant." Bob was putting down a few names, and finding suitable places and times that afternoon when I could meet some of the students and get acquainted.

"How about a time with Tom?" I suggested. "Find out if he has a free period this afternoon. I'd like to talk with him."

I met Tom at three in the student lounge. It was one of those long old army barracks reconditioned for campuses which grew too fast. I had looked forward to this meeting. I wanted to know Tom and know how he felt about things. One thing I did realize: He wanted to do the art work for this Christian club.

We sat side by side in the narrow old building. After the usual get-acquainted talk, I asked a few questions. I found him easy to talk to, and quite open. I wanted to find out what he thought about Jesus Christ, and where *He* was in Tom's thinking, but I hesitated to barge in.

"Tom, you seem to like this Inter-Varsity group."

"Yes, I really do. I like them."

"Do you like to hear them sing and talk about Jesus Christ?"

"Yes, I do. I really enjoy it when we're singing and talking together."

That told me so much about Tom that I decided to do a little barging.

"Tom, you know what I heard about you this noon?"

"No, what?"

"That you're a fine art chairman but the kids aren't sure if you're a Christian or not."

I waited for his answer, hoping I hadn't gone too far. Tom bowed his head and there was a silence.

"That's right. I'm not a Christian." And then he added, "But I wish I were."

During this conversation I was remembering the freshness of John 6:44 which had so recently opened its meaning to me. "No one can come to me unless the Father who sent me draws him. . . ." (RSV). A wondrous thing: the word *draw*. "To attract, to allure, to cause to come or follow; as a magnet." Those who come to Christ are drawn ones, drawn by the Father Himself.

I was feeling the drawing power. The Father was drawing Tom's heart to Jesus Christ. But he didn't know it. He didn't understand what was happening to him. He only knew that he wanted to be with people who loved and believed in Christ.

"You know," he continued, "I think a lot about being a Christian. Sometimes in my room when I'm alone at night, I'd give anything if I knew I belonged to Jesus Christ."

"Tom, who do you think put that idea into your head? Where do you think it came from?"

"You mean wanting to be a Christian? Well, I guess my mother had something to do with it when I was a little boy. And I know my Sunday school teacher, and the pastor of our church have helped. Yes, I know they have."

"Who else, Tom, could have put the thought of being a Christian into your head?"

He looked at me as I began to turn through my New Testament to John 6. We read, "No one can come to me unless the Father who sent me draws him . . ." (John 6:44, RSV). "All that the Father gives me will come to me; and him who comes to me I will not cast out" (John 6:37, RSV). "For this is the will of my Father, that every one who sees the Son and believes in him should have eternal life; and I will raise him up at the last day . . . I am the bread of life; he who comes to me shall not hunger, and he who believes in me shall never thirst" (John 6:40, 35, RSV).

We read it carefully. We read it again.

Who can come to the Lord Jesus? Every one whom the Father is drawing.

Who can come to the Lord Jesus? Every one whose heart the Father has opened to want to believe in Christ.

Who can come to the Lord Jesus? Every one who finds a response in his heart to the Father's invitation to come.

In other words, any person who finds a desire in his heart to know about God is responding. Response is the first step. How dynamic that definition is for the one who is moving out of the darkness of unbelief into the light of faith.

"Tom, it's the great love of the Father-God who put this desire into your heart, through your mother, your Sunday school teacher, your pastor. God loves you. He has been drawing you toward Himself all this time. He wants you."

Tom leaned forward so far that his head almost touched his knees. In the stillness that followed I was amazed to see sudden tears fall. In a moment he straightened up, pulled out his handkerchief, blew his nose and said, "Well, I guess in my heart I was a believer in Christ all the time. Only I didn't know it until now."

We thanked God. What else was there to do? After all, a gift had been given. "Coming to Jesus" means response — from the heart first and then the lips and life. I saw Tom every time I returned to the campus. He was no longer a secret, unknown believer but an open, radiant follower of Jesus Christ.

When does life begin? From the physical standpoint, if there is no life at birth, it's too late. From the spiritual viewpoint, life begins with signs of God's Spirit at work. "Coming to Jesus" means recognizing that He is a Living Person with whom we may speak about our relationship to Him and about everything in life. "Son, go in peace. Daughter, go in peace. Your faith in Me has made you a whole person."

For Discussion

1. Discuss and memorize: John 6:35, 44.
2. From the last two paragraphs of chapter 1, and the first two paragraphs of chapter 2, find at least six definitions of a Christian. Discuss: what God does, and what we do.
3. Why is the question: Who can become a Christian? more provocative than: How to become a Christian?
4. List the signs which indicate that a person is "becoming" a Christian.

Prayer Time

Silently Quietly, now go through the definitions from No. 2 (above) and apply them personally.

Audibly Give thanks for those ideas which have the most meaning to you at this time. Offer praise and worship to our Saviour, Jesus Christ, who made all this possible.

15

How Much Does One Need to Believe?

Becoming a Christian, or being a Christian, is a matter of belief.

Belief in what?
How much faith does a person need?
How much Christian doctrine must he understand in order to assure himself that he's actually a Christian?

Confusion over these questions lies in the hearts of many sincere people. Some call themselves Christian when deep in their hearts they know they're afraid to examine such questions lest their insecurity be uncovered. Others feel assured that they once believed in the Lord Jesus Christ, but because of continued failure they torment themselves that they're not really Christians at all. And then there are those with longing hearts (Jesus calls this being hungry and thirsty) who feel they *could* know for sure, if only they knew *what* to believe.

The present question is, How much Christian doctrine is it necessary to know to become a Christian?

Offhand, someone might answer, The more you know, the better. This isn't always true. Many unbelievers know all the doctrinal beliefs of Christianity, and yet they won't call themselves Christian.

When I was in high school, a tent evangelist in our little North Dakota town told us a story about a North American Indian chief who wanted to become a Christian. He thought he had to pray in English to be saved, and so he prayed all the English he knew: "Dear God, a, b, c, d, e, f, g, Amen." And God saved him.

The requisite of being a Christian seems to lie somewhere between the yielding heart-attitude of the one who is speaking to God, and the fact that he has faith in God.

Someone will quickly say, "Believe on the Lord Jesus and you will be saved." Believe what? Or shall we say, believe whom? Jesus Christ or God? Can a person be saved without calling on Jesus Christ?

Shirley, a very intelligent Jewish girl, whose Christian friend had long loved and prayed for her, came to a crisis in her life and found herself praying. Devouring the New Testament for the first time, she found that everything spoke to her. Purpose in life, new attitudes, newness of heart, were all hers. In a few weeks' time, she discovered that the God she actually believed in and worshiped was Jesus Christ. Her first belief was in God as she knew Him, and then she was led to God as He had revealed Himself in the New Testament. "Every one who has heard and learned from the Father comes to me" (John 6:45, RSV). "All that the Father gives me will come to me; and him who comes to me I will not cast out" (John 6:37, RSV).

Your honest search for truth will compel you to ask and knock and seek until the door is opened to you. And there *is* Someone on the other side of the door. In fact, He Himself said, "I am the door; if any one enters by me, he will be saved, and will go in and out and find pasture" (John 10:9, RSV).

"Believe in the Lord Jesus, and you will be saved . . ." (Acts 16:31, RSV). What shall we believe about Him? "Believe that He died for your sins," comes another answer. This is so true. Yet some people hear this message, repeat it, and even say that they believe it, but nothing happens. They aren't changed. Some may begin to conform, but nothing is really different.

Believing in a person means trusting his integrity, relying upon him. And this is what believing in the Lord Jesus is. We can distinguish between two aspects of belief: first of all, *who He is;* and then, *what He has done.* For years, I had the order reversed.

I'd been a Christian since high school, later a missionary in China, and then a staff member for Inter-Varsity Christian Fellowship before the whole wonderful truth of the atonement finally began to break upon me. And it broke with real excitement. The ever-increasing light of what the cross meant, and what Christ did there, began to open and unfold.

I saw that the plan of salvation was Christ-centered, not salvation-centered. I saw with astonishment that the gospel isn't, "If you'll confess your sins, believe on the Lord Jesus, make restitution and be separate from the world, you'll be saved." The Gospel is, "Man, what are you waiting for? Jesus Christ has taken care of the sin question on the cross. It is finished." This is the best news anyone could ever hear. This is the good news.

I worked out a logical question-and-answer sheet with a diagram. I explained it to anyone who would listen to me. I kept adding more things, as more truth unfolded, and had Scripture verses ready to use when necessary. I felt that if people understood everything about the atonement, and why Christ had to die, they would have a good foundation of truth for their belief.

But again that question arose. What is essential? How much does one have to believe to be saved? Was all that explanation necessary? I was beginning to be open for the Spirit to teach me about the *Person of Christ* as well as *the work of Christ.*

Rereading the third chapter of John, I noticed Jesus' words about the new life and how it comes. He compared the working of God's Spirit in a human heart to the capricious blowing of the wind. We see the results of what the wind does, but no one knows where it comes from and where it goes. So it is with the Holy Spirit. We can't lead another person to Christ by stating how much or how little he has to believe. Only the Holy Spirit can gently and quietly open a man's heart to receive the life of God. And who is to say by what means? Or at what time? God made the heart and knows that above all we need to know the security of being loved and being loving. And only He knows how to open our heart.

This is why God Himself had to come to earth in the Person of Jesus Christ. This is why the new life He gives to us has to do with what we believe about Christ. Not how much we believe, nor how much we understand about Him, but *what we believe about Him.*

"Who are You, Lord?" Saul asked.

"I am Jesus," came the answer, as the light flashed through Saul's educated mind. From that moment Saul became Paul, the willing disciple of Jesus Christ, instead of the cruel, determined persecutor of the early Christians.

There is no given formula for what you are to believe. But belief is never stated in the New Testament as having to do with "belief that your sins are forgiven." If you look up all the passages with the word "faith" you will find that they have to do with belief in the Person of Jesus Christ. Who He is: this is first in importance. What He did: this is next — for what He did has no significance apart from who He is.

"Give your heart to Jesus Christ," comes the invitation.

"Who is He that I might give myself to Him?" comes the response.

Giving up your heart and self to God: this brings God Himself right into your heart. Giving up only your sins to Him: this is an experience of forgiveness which brings the fresh air of heaven into your heart.

Either of these steps will result in a sense of assurance. But danger lies in taking only the second, centering on what happens to yourself. If your attention is on the first, you will be centering on Jesus Christ (God in the flesh). The result will be that you have given yourself to a Person, not to a doctrine or experience. And of course, along with the Person of Christ, you also receive the forgiveness of your sins.

"My son, your sins are forgiven," Jesus said to the paralyzed man in Mark 2:5, RSV, thus giving Himself in a personal relationship first of all, and then stating the meaning of that relationship (which is forgiveness).

This brings us to the statement that belief isn't primarily intellectual, for mere mental assent can be cold acknowledgement. Belief is primarily an act of the heart — warm, living, personal. Only when our emotions have been touched will our volitional powers reach out to grasp what our intellect is beginning to perceive.

How much does a person need to believe to become a Christian? Are you checking up on yourself as you read, perhaps looking for some mention of the way or means by which you became a Christian? By whatever means you have found Christ, you can be sure it is satisfactory with Him. If you haven't yet found Him, you can be certain of one thing: He is seeking you. And when you are "found of Him" you will know it.

Ask yourself this question: "What do I believe about Jesus Christ?"

"Who are you?" the religious people in Matthew's Gospel were constantly asking Jesus. "Who do you believe yourself to be?" Upon the identity and authority of this miracle-working Teacher hung all the authenticity of what He was doing and saying.

You can look upon Him as the Saviour who died for the sins of the world but be certain you respond to Him as *your* Saviour. He died for *your* sins.

And be sure to look upon Him as "the image of the invisible God . . . for . . . all things were created through him and for him" (Colossians 1:15, 16, RSV). " ' . . . For the secret is very near you, in your own heart, in your own mouth!' It is the secret of faith . . . 'If you openly admit . . . that Jesus Christ is the Lord, and if you believe in your own heart that God raised him from the dead, you will be saved.' For,

Whosoever shall call upon the name of the Lord shall be saved" (Romans 10:8-10, 13, *Phillips*).

Believe that Jesus Christ is the Lord, Let your heart fall on its knees. Look into His face and call on His name: "Lord Jesus. You are my Lord." Believe that He is the God who died and who is now alive. You may add other words of thanksgiving or contrition, but primarily let your kneeling heart worship Him as your Lord and your God, now and forever.

For Discussion

1. Memorize John 10:9.
2. Discuss the story of Tom in chapter 2. How much did he need to believe? When did his belief start?
3. What is the good news (in a capsule) which we must share with others?
4. Set up a dialogue situation; let two discuss while the others evaluate (and discuss it later). (Subject: The difference between *the Work of Christ* and *the Person of Christ*. Use everyday language. Omit religious cliches. Learn to speak to those unfamiliar with church language.
5. How is Jesus the Door? How does a person take this step of going "through" a door?

Prayer Time

Silently Worship. Give thanks. Meditate on the last paragraph.

Audibly Acknowledge with thanksgiving your growing relationship with Jesus Christ; or any other truth you became aware of today.

16

Growing As a Christian: New Goals

> *The kingdom of heaven is like something precious buried in a field, which a man found and hid again; then in his joy he goes and sells all he has and buys that field* (Matthew 13:44, *Amplified*).

IN CONSIDERING the new goals of the Christian's life, I have not intended to outline specifics, such as: What is my life work? Who will be my life-partner? How will I know which church to belong to? What is the dividing line between right and wrong? In some religions you have a guidebook to tell you *exactly* what you may or may not do, but not in the Christian religion. A new heart is placed within you, a heart to know the Shepherd's voice. A new spirit is within you, the Spirit of our Lord and Christ, to guide and teach you.

Actually, this is the difference between the Old and the New Testaments. In the Old, there were definite and set laws with myriads of smaller rules for interpreting them correctly, and strong penalties for all known infractions. In the New, the rigidity of the Old Testament law is fulfilled in a new birth and a new spirit (Jeremiah 31:31, 33), so that love can be the motivation in every circumstance. And what about the offenders? They soon find out that when they break the Royal Law of Love, they break themselves.

Many new Christians are not clearly aware of the new goals in life. The following suggested goals are given as principles which will help you find the lesser ones which make up daily living. Each day is a new beginning. The lesser goals will change from time to time, as your spiritual eyesight grows clearer, while the greater goals will shine more clearly and brightly with greater meaning as you yourself are being stretched and enlarged.

THE FIRST GOAL: KNOW HIS IDENTITY

The first goal, after meeting your Lord face-to-face, is to know more about Him. *To know who He really is.*

Do you know who Christ really is? It was when the Apostle Paul discovered who Christ was, that he was converted. However, this revelation sometimes comes after a person has made his commitment.

Paul was traveling to Damascus with an armed party, fully equipped and authorized to arrest all the Christians he could find, and deliver them to the authorities, where they would be tried and executed for treason. So great was his conviction that Christians were enemies to the historical religion of his fathers, the Jehovah God of Abraham, Isaac, and Jacob, that he gave himself wholly to this task.

As he traveled on that dusty road, ". . . suddenly a light from heaven flashed around him, And he fell to the ground. Then he heard a voice saying to him, Saul, Saul, why are you persecuting Me? . . . And Saul said, Who are You, Lord? And He said, I am Jesus, Whom you are persecuting. . . . Trembling and astonished he asked, Lord, what do You desire me to do?" (Acts 9:3-6, *Amplified*).

Meeting Jesus Christ is a life-changing experience for anyone. After that, people seem different, you yourself will be different. In reality, things are pretty much the same as ever, the difference is that Christ has moved into the control room of your heart and taken over. You are beginning to see things from His viewpoint.

"Lord, who are you?" were Saul's first words, as he encountered the presence of Christ. (Saul's name later was changed to Paul). The answer was revealing, there was no mistaking who it was, "I am Jesus, Whom you are persecuting."

So the Christians were right. The Jesus of the Christians is one with the great Jehovah of the Old Testament! He did come to be the Living Word among mankind.

Now the second illustration:

C.S., who made her personal commitment to Christ a few months ago, finally found out who He really is. She writes: "Just ten minutes ago, nearly two centuries away, Jesus finally won! For the first time in my life, I have been extremely sensitive to all our Lord's suffering as a human being. Until recently I regarded Him as Someone apart from humanity, One given to special divinity and immune from earthly cares. Now I know *without question* that this is not true. He is real! As a real person, He died that we may be saved. One Sunday at church I had to control my tears when the full realization broke, of what that Holy Week meant in relation to His crucifixion. How fortunate I am to have this truth. With each assailing doubt, God makes Himself, through Jesus, more and more real to me. A wonderful experience, this *growing in Christ*."

This is the truth which the whole New Testament seeks to make plain, yet it is only when the Holy Spirit opens our heart to understand, that we know the truth personally.

> *At the beginning God expressed himself. That personal expression, that word, was with God, and was God, and he existed with God from the beginning. . . . So the word of God became a human being and lived among us* (John 1:1, 2, 14, *Phillips*).

Has this truth been revealed to you? Do you know who the permanent Guest in your heart is? You may think you do, but there is always more. The other goals will help us to know more about how this revelation takes place.

THE SECOND GOAL: LOVE HIM

The second goal is to know more about Christ as we learn to *love Him.* For everything positive about the new life can be said in these two commandments:

> *The Lord our God is one Lord, and you shall love the Lord your God with your whole heart, with your whole soul, with your whole mind and with your whole strength. . . . You shall love your neighbor as yourself* (Mark 12:29, 31, *Berkeley*).

Loving God means loving ourselves and loving others as well as loving Him. Forgiveness and acceptance are all wrapped up together in this wonderful package, because they are a part of love.

How can you learn to love the Lord your God? Get acquainted with Jesus Christ, as the first goal suggested. The Holy Spirit puts the love of God into your hearts, God's kind of love (Romans 5:8). We are able to love because God is love. We don't have to pump up love, it is a gift to us.

We need to accept love and to give love. We do this in human love by small, intimate things. We please the one we love. We call him by name. We like to be with him.

We can show our love to Jesus Christ by the same small intimate things. In chapter 20 we'll be talking about hearing Him speak to us, so we can know the things that please Him.

One of the things that pleases us, is to be called by our name. Most of us are quite particular about that name, for it is our own peculiar property. We like to have people say it, and say it correctly. We also have various "little" names which are only for intimate circles — family or close friends.

Now that you have met Christ, what are you calling

Him? Or is His name difficult to say, for reasons known only to yourself? Jesus is His historical name. Jesus Christ is His religious name. To those who love Him, He is known as Master, Saviour, Lord, Lord Jesus, Lord Jesus Christ. By your own permission He has now become Saviour, Lord and Master in your heart and life. There is a certain power in the very saying of His name, taking His name upon your lips, addressing Him. I love this old hymn:

> Take the Name of Jesus with you,
> Child of sorrow and of woe,
> It will joy and comfort give you,
> Take it then where e'er you go.
> Precious Name, O how sweet,
> Hope of earth and joy of heaven.

What meaning does His name have for you? By what name do you call Him? This One who loved you and gave Himself for you.

THE THIRD GOAL: MAKE HIM LORD

The third goal is to know more about Jesus Christ, not only in Name and in Person and by loving Him, but by *making Him Lord*, indeed.

Remember the story of Saul on the Damascus Road? His first question was, "Who are You, Lord?" As soon as he found out, He put *the* important word where it belonged, "*Lord*, what do you want me to do?" Instinctively, before he asked the question, he must have known who it was; but deliberately he said, "*Lord*, what do you want me to do?" I hope you have read the whole chapter of Acts 9, because we're going to be referring to it again in Chapter 20, and you'll see how Paul literally did what he was told to do.

Paul's first question was one of astonished incredulity — Can this Jesus be Lord? His second question was one of complete submission, born of certainty as well as of recognition — Lord, here I am, just tell me what You want me to do, and I'm ready. He was ready to do what he formerly would have despised to do: join himself to the Christians, because his immediate encounter with Jesus Christ made him one of them.

When you've found Jesus as your Saviour. He also becomes your Lord, whether you are aware of it or not. If you aren't at first, you soon will be. His name is the Lord Jesus Christ, and He does not come to us in partial entities of Himself. Because of our limited knowledge, we sometimes think He does, as we give more and more of ourselves to Him.

When you've found Jesus as Saviour, He is also the Lord, the Master, the One who can control you right from your inner being. He is the One to whom you belong. Immediately you are ready to do His will — if only you know what it is. You are ready to hear and obey, "Lord, what do You want me to do?"

It is important that right from the start you recognize the Lordship of Christ, and that He (not well-meaning people) is directing you. Whatever anyone else says about Him, or tells you to do, first go quietly to Him, "Lord, what do You want me to do?"

There are many schools of "victorious life" teaching, and I've experienced most of them. They helped me, but in the end I've come to know that Jesus, my Lord, is my victorious life; not some surrender of mine, nor some teaching about how things should work. After my first book, *The Years That Count*, came out, a professor from a certain seminary wrote a review of the book. His viewpoint did not agree with mine as stated. He felt I had confused an important issue in the last chapter — that of Jesus as Saviour and Jesus as Lord, which he pointed out does not come at the time because one is unable as yet to comprehend such a truth. The viewpoint I expressed has come through personal experience, as well as years of careful study of the Scriptures and contacts with others in whose lives God is working. I've had to be open to learn more of His ways to keep my Christian life fresh and growing.

How can we separate the name of our Lord Jesus?

He is the Lord and Saviour, Jesus Christ. Accept as much of Him as you know today, and give as much of yourself as you know, today. When you know more, you can give more and accept more. This principle works gloriously and practically in the lives of new Christians. Don't withhold anything — give everything. Lord, what will You have me to do?

THE FOURTH GOAL: READ

This goal concerns your spiritual growth, and it will also help you reach toward the other three goals.

The best source for learning more about Christ is from your Bible. There you will find what Jesus Christ said, what He is like, and how others reacted to Him. Store it away in your heart by reading every day. Become familiar with it by re-reading. Through its pages, the Holy Spirit will teach you many things you need to know.

Here are several specific suggestions which can help you to a good start in your daily devotional life.

1. Regarding devotional books: There are many good books and pamphlets. You can step into any Christian book store and find them. No matter how good a devotional book may be, it can never replace your Bible.

2. Start reading the New Testament regularly. Look at the fly leaf of your Bible. What kind of a Bible is it? Is it the King James Version, in Shakespearean English? If it is, may I suggest that you will be greatly benefited if you secure at least one more Bible — one of the newer translations which makes reading easier and the meaning clearer. Compare the two. This will sharpen your perception. Perhaps you've noticed I've used several translations in this book, so we might always have the clearest possible meaning.

The reason for the difference is that the original Greek is a fluid language with words for every possible shade of meaning, while English, in comparison, is a sharp, hard language with limited meaning for words.

When you are reading the gospels, will you try this suggestion? Be there with Christ and His disciples. Discipline your mind, your imagination, and be there. Even if you take only one paragraph at a sitting. If you need to take an imaginary name, and be one of the persons in the crowd, do it — get right into the situation. Live in it. See and hear and smell and feel, what they experienced. Until you are living in those days, walking with the Master, listening and observing, you'll never really know what it means to let the Bible speak to you.

When the Bible speaks to you, it is as the written Word. When the Spirit of God speaks to you in your heart, it is as the living Word. Jesus Christ is both the written Word and the Living Word, He *is* the Word. He is contained in the Word. He never contradicts Himself. You must learn of Him, about Him, and from Him.

3. For those who wish a study guide (as I do), I strongly recommend the quarterly study notes for Bible reading, published in small booklets for various age groups, by The Scripture Union Bible Study, 239 Fairfield Avenue, Upper Darby, Pa. 19082. They'll gladly send you samples upon request.

4. Include one of the Psalms each time you read, for through them you will learn to pray. Read aloud to yourself, read it as a prayer, as your prayer. When you are ready you can begin to read the Old Testament.

5. Learn to pray by praying. Most people like to have a set time for prayer and Bible reading, but when you miss, don't go around condemning yourself. When you keep it, enjoy it, and meet your Lord there. Christ is in you and with you. In time, you'll have a running conversation with Him all day long. He's ready to help you in little things as well as big things. Here again, you can find practical books on prayer which will help you, which in turn you can recommend to others.

I have suggested four goals. Why not list some more

for yourself? Talk it over with your Lord first. Ask Him about new goals for various areas of your life. You can even list the old ones with the new ones, and rejoice as you note your new growth. Writing things down makes goals clearer. Then put them away, tuck them in your Bible. When you find them again, check things over to find what you've been learning. See if what you've written has been in line with what Christ is teaching you. Make revisions, make changes, make additions. Remember what's right for you is not necessarily right (at this time) for another; and what's right for others now, is not necessarily right for you at this time. We are not to judge one another, but to love and pray for one another.

In varying degrees, as you grow in this new life with Christ, you'll want to meet with other Christians, to attend a church where you can participate in true worship, to attend a Bible study class, to receive Holy Communion, and to give of your means as God has given to you. When you do any of these things, talk it over with Christ, know what He wants you to do. Then you will be serving Him from your heart, and this is well-pleasing in His sight.

Just as in human friendship, we reveal ourselves slowly to one another, so our Saviour reveals Himself, bit by bit, as we are ready. There are exciting discoveries about Him to be made which last a life-time. The Treasure you have will be unveiled more and more, and the influence of Christ within you will be more and more personalized.

For you are the child of His love.

For Discussion

1. Read Matthew 13:44. Colossians 1:15-20, 2:1-10, *Phillips*. Read these aloud, and devote a few minutes to discussion. How do these ideas help us fulfill some of our goals.
2. Write down the four goals in this chapter, leaving ample space beneath each one.
3. Under each goal, list things every Christian should know. Arrive at these through reading this chapter, discussion, memory, experience.

Prayer Time

Silently Using the above material, underline that which pertains to you. Try to select goals which can be reached within a week, two weeks, a month, two months. Make them simple enough so they can be carried out.

Audibly Let your thanksgiving and your petitions follow the subjects you have been working on during the silent period. Pray for yourself, using the pronoun "I" so that others also may pray for you.

17

The Place of Failure in a Christian's Life

MANY PEOPLE HAVE TOLD ME that before they became Christians they had scarcely any problems. Now it seems that either they have a problem, are a problem or live with a problem.

The Gospel is not a success story, but a story of victory in failure. It is false to preach this as the Gospel: "Receive Christ and live happily ever after." Jesus Christ was wonderful, not in His success but in His failure. Not in His happiness, but in His despair. The disciple is not above His Master. Since Jesus Christ became obedient through the things He suffered, what right do we have to retreat from problem situations, or to play ostrich and pretend that they don't exist?

How much conflict do you have? Are you in conflict with organized Christianity, with social standards? Or is your conflict rooted in inner guilt because of your repeated failures? Has life handed you problems from which no escape seems possible?

The interpretation of failure depends on your point of view. There is a big difference between "being" and "doing."

According to most men who knew Jesus, His life was a failure. Only a few knew the truth of His resurrection. This is what the incarnation is all about: that God living in a human body was quietly expanding His kingdom in the hearts of men who seemed to be failures.

Man looks on the outward appearance, while God looks on the heart. To look at your failure from God's point of view is important.

In whose eyes have you failed? If you quietly consider His viewpoint, your wavering will cease and your faith will begin to grow long roots of stability. God sees the whole person, the whole pattern. In His eyes, seeming failure is part of the growth process. In His sight even some of our successes need to be redeemed — and can be.

For some years I was greatly disturbed because I felt I had the wrong kind of problems. My failures weren't the kind that Jesus had. I was mentally dividing failure into two categories: the kind God uses for my good, and the kind where my own foolish stupidity involved me with the consequences. These I felt I had to take care of myself. Sometimes my failures seemed to be justified by the circumstances. But other times I felt vaguely that they could be called sin by someone else, because they stemmed from wrong attitudes.

God doesn't separate failure into such neatly bound categories. He works with the whole person. His redemption works in all that we are and all that we do.

More is to be faced in failure than the failure itself. Failure inevitably results in guilt, which can be more depressing and dangerous than the failure. Some of the guilt resulting from failure undoubtedly is false guilt. We expect ourselves to do the impossible. God does not. Therefore we need to weigh our circumstances realistically. One of my friends looks for a physical reason when depression overtakes her; and if she is too tired, she deducts 80 per cent of her concern. Another friend believes that about 90 per cent of our difficulties are caused by lack of maturity and poor judgment. If we have realized that this is true, we can rejoice in the fact that we have seen our need for more maturity, thank God for the failure and stop feeling guilty.

Attempting to define failure helped to open a wide door to maturity for me. For years as a young Christian, I blamed everything on the devil. This was partly due to the teaching I received: that sin is only a deliberate act of the will. And since I always avoided the deliberate *choice* to sin, I told myself that the consequences of my actions were merely due to a "mistake," and that God understood my heart motives. As I grew older, I learned that maturity develops when one makes a choice and is prepared to accept the responsibility connected with it.

To know how to face failure honestly, to find the cause, to be willing for God's remedy, is the next step.

Sometimes honesty is painful, but it is essential before failure can be made a constructive part of life. As long as I was blaming the devil or some other person, I was failing in the worst possible sense. I was refusing to take responsibility for my acts and attitudes.

I also began to learn the difference between a blanket sense of guilt (which came from the accuser, the devil) and the specific sense of guilt (which came when God's spirit pointed out sin). The latter, I could do something about.

I still tended to rationalize, though. "Lord, if I've hurt my brother, if I have any resentment, if I have any hurt pride, if I was wrong, if I was standing on my own rights, if, if, if." The day came when I turned that *if* into a declarative sentence of confession. "Lord, I know I hurt my brother this morning by my thoughtlessness. It was just plain selfishness. I was only thinking of myself. Forgive me for the cruel things I said." Before the day was over, I asked my brother's forgiveness too.

Honesty pays dividends. After I had asked forgiveness the thought came: "What I said was true, but it wasn't loving. The trouble lay in the way I said it." A light went on. I began to see.

The reason for depression and discouragement was now cleared. Emotional distress often results from unconsciously moving away from God. Demanding "understanding" or certain advantages and privileges has only one end, the tangible promotion of self.

That is why I would add self-control to the list of things needed to make a failure creative. Self-control is one of the results of love. And love is the motivation which balances and stabilizes, and waits with patience for fulfilling the law. Self-control results from God-control. "Thou shalt love the Lord thy God with all thy heart."

The paradox of life in Christ is that we're not conscious of our holiness, but more and more conscious of our short-comings. This is cause not for despair but for thanksgiving. We can discern where we fail and expose ourselves more fully to God's love. This is the process which theologians call sanctification.

As we sense our failure we must look to the cross. The crucifixion of felons was Rome's most ignominious punishment. By His quiet acceptance of the cross when He had done no wrong, Jesus Christ creatively and redemptively took care of all sin and wrong-doing, which separates man from God. How this was possible cannot be comprehended. Read the story for yourself with an open heart. It will be revealed to you according to your need.

Forgiveness restores that which has previously been separated. Separation is pain. Grace is the wide liberty that frees us from separation and pain, and enables God to help us make creative use of all our failures.

Dr. Paul Tournier says: "He who has tasted grace can no longer be content with compromises, escapism, of psychological compensation. He is constrained to confront all life's problems courageously and faithfully to do battle with them. Grace gives us the victory over our nature, but it does not suppress nature; it restores the flow of life which sets us free. Even so, complete freedom will be ours only beyond death and resurrection" (*The Meaning of Persons*, Tournier, Harper, 1957, p. 14).

Though we live in a perpetual state of incompleteness, we can live in a constant state of dependence upon our Lord and His loving acceptance. The redemptive love of God is continually operative in His beloved world.

For Discussion

1. Read I John 1:7. Matthew 6:22-24.
2. What are the reasons for discouragement or depression? What should one look for first?
3. Define: failure, true and false guilt, rationalization, maturity.
4. What are the easy ways "out" of failure? What important aspect of the Christian life are we thwarting?
5. List 5 or 6 positive things which will help you to incorporate new attitudes into your conscious and unconscious mind.
6. What paradox do we constantly face? So then, what should our daily attitude be?

Prayer Time

Silently

In these areas, meditate on how you may face failure creatively (with courage, and without depression).

a. When you feel you have failed God.
b. When you have failed in personal relationships.
c. When you fail to face up to yourself.

Audibly

For confession: go back to No. 3 above.
For asking and receiving: go back to No. 4.
Ask members of the group to quote prayer promises.

18

How Different Should a Christian Be?

"YES, I WANT TO GIVE my heart to Jesus Christ, but . . ." Terri hesitated and then continued, "I'm a chain smoker, and I like my beer."

We were in a national park, looking out over the jagged white tops of the Rockies. Terri was employed by the state social service department, and had come to the Christian conference with her boy friend for just one day.

In effect she was saying, "With these things hanging onto me, people could never approve of me, and I could never be perfect enough to be a Christian. I'm willing to give up anything Christ opposes, but I just don't have the will power."

How much will I have to give up? This question can confuse the whole issue of becoming a Christian. A decision must be made, but let's try to see just where Terri's choice lay.

To illustrate, I picked up two books. "Terri, this blue book in my left hand represents your compulsion toward cigarettes and beer. This red book in my right hand represents your desire toward Jesus Christ. Now listen carefully: your choice isn't between these two. You don't have to control your compulsion *before* you receive Christ, regardless of what you may think or what you've been told. Right now, your choice isn't 'either-or.' This is your choice" — and I put my left hand and the blue book behind me out of sight, and held out the red book which represents Jesus Christ. "You are going to say 'Yes' to Christ or 'No' to Christ. Your choice is whether or not to give Him your heart."

"But what about giving up —" Terri began.

"Now wait. The heart motive always comes first. Do you really want Jesus Christ to control your life? Because if you do, He'll tell you what to do and then give you the strength to do it. He'll free you from your compulsion *after* you have received Him, not before."

Terri gave her heart to Christ that day, more than ten years ago, and since then she has continued to learn that Christian perfection, as well as separation from the world, concerns motivation before conduct.

How separate should you be from earth-things and earth-people in order to be an authentic Christian? How much does your own fulfillment depend upon what you do, what you have to give up, or the choices you make? And how are you to determine what Christian people want you to do, and what God wants you to do?

If self is at the controls of your life, you'll soon find that outward influences (the approval of the Christian group to which you belong, for instance, or the desire to impress your non-Christian friends) may dictate your behavior more strongly than you realize. Becoming a Christian means that you've willingly asked Jesus Christ to take over the controls. He will show you the real issues and how to meet them. He met them, too, when He lived on earth.

As a growing child of God, you'll sometimes recognize in yourself a see-saw tendency to go from one extreme to the other — from pleasing people, to pleasing God, to pleasing people. You find that your behavior is a variable which operates according to both the judgments of those watching you and the motives of your heart, until through experience and quiet prayer you begin to level out.

The presence of Christ in your heart means that a living Person will guide you and be with you and help you evaluate and choose, according to His will for you.

However, you'll soon discover that your heart has two faces which seem to demand a certain satisfaction.

Both seem to put up good arguments which find reinforcement at every turn.

One side of your heart seems to say, "This is a wonderful new world. You should live this new life so that everyone can see you're a follower of Christ. You want to be as 'perfect' a Christian as it's possible to be." (This is right, for in one sense a Christian does have the reputation of Jesus Christ in his hands).

Then comes the subtle question from the other side of your heart: how "perfect" should you be? You can't be really perfect, because only God is perfect. And you don't see any perfect Christians, do you? Anyway, what you want to do seems right, so how can it be wrong for you — even if it might be wrong for your brother?

In other words, your clever heart is asking, "How can you arrange things so that you can do what you want, and still be in the right?" Bluntly, "What can I get by with?"

With whom are you trying to get by? With God? Other people? Yourself?

In the face of these devious possibilities, I find that a prayer for help arises from my heart: "Dear Lord, help me to think straight. Help me to think Your thoughts. Deliver me from protecting myself. Deliver me from the fear of people. Teach me Your ways. Teach me the simple, plain truths about Christian growth and maturity."

Before we examine the potential for God's kind of perfection, and the goals and factors which help or hinder, let's try to define what is meant by the term, "Christian perfection."

Most people will agree that outward separation from questionable things isn't Christian perfection. Rather the heart with all its motives or intentions must be perfect before God. People will always be sitting on the judgment-seat no matter what you do, so you have to examine your real motives and live for God's approval because only He knows your heart.

This is fine. But sooner or later those on the judgment-seat (and who isn't?) will begin to tell you that your heart is being molded by what you do, and therefore it's necessary to have some controls. Then when they see your outward conformity, they take it as proof that your heart is "perfect" in its intentions. The mad race is on, and we're back where we started: those who are the "most separated" (from outward things that are worldly and sinful) are the most "spiritual."

It is true that when we consciously or unconsciously play an outward role, we are inwardly affected. On the other hand, the reverse is also true. When Christ lives *in* us, He affects our outward behavior. Authentic behavior is based on a balance of the inward and the outward.

Is sounds unbelievable now, but when I was converted as a fifteen-year-old, thirty years before the hippies, it was a mark of spirituality to wear long black stockings, long sleeves, long hair and absolutely no jewelry or make-up (although it's also true that I was required to sign no card promising to abstain from certain worldly things). But times have changed. Things which were considered sinful then, such as movies, are today found in almost every home on the TV screen. And today anyone can wear black stockings.

But what about our *inner* selves? What about the love for others which should characterize Christians? What rascals we're making of each other when we demand outward conformity and don't demand the proof of the inner attitude of love in our relationship with others. We're playing the role of people-pleasers. Now it's true that what we do outwardly deeply affects us inwardly. But this kind of perfectionism is decor, a kind of outward white-washing, which leaves the inside untouched. Jesus severely condemned the Pharisees for their outward attention to rules and their "perfection" devoid of love. He said, "Be ye perfect, as your heavenly Father is perfect." If you carefully reread the Sermon on the Mount, you'll find that He was contrasting human relationships based on law (which is rigid) with those based on love (which goes the second mile).

Perfectness in love is a wholeness which affects our whole personality. This perfect love is a result of Christ's presence in our hearts, for He is love. And His love is ours to have and make use of. Perfectness in love is also a wholeness that results from spiritual growth, and from having one's senses exercised by discerning good from evil.

Christian maturity is a relative perfectness which has flexibility, movement, rhythm. It is an adjusting to people and to circumstances. This kind of spiritual living isn't reached or regulated by rigid rules today, any more than it was in the days of our Lord.

Christian maturity doesn't sit on the judgment-seat which is Christ's alone. Christian maturity sits on the love-seat, and leaves others to the One who is both Lover and Judge by right of His death on the cross. He knows the human heart, and He never judges by appearances.

Christian maturity (perfection) operates by loving God with the whole heart, mind, soul and strength.

Christian maturity enables a person to take pleasure in all his gifts without being the slave of any; to accept each circumstances that arises, to face all the problems it raises, and to listen to what God is saying through it.

The desire for authentic Christian perfection doesn't center on ourselves or in our spiritual progress. Rather it turns outward as His did, manifesting itself in nothing that is antagonistic to holy love.

Christ's love in our hearts releases us from the rigidity which binds, to the freedom which operates by love. This is the love that motivated Him when He broke the Pharisees' "laws" to meet the needs of troubled people.

For Discussion

1. Read and discuss: Colossians 2:16-23 (*Amplified*).
2. What was Terri's false supposition? Her true choice?
3. How can one determine whether he is being unduly influenced by people, or whether he is pleasing God? What is the third alternative?
4. Discuss motivation and conduct. Which comes first? Why?
5. Name five attitudes which a maturing Christian should attempt to bring into his life.

Prayer Time

Silently Am I demanding from others some conformity which contradicts my own secret life?
Am I attempting to "get by" with something, when it definitely hurts my brother?

Audibly (Choose one of the following for your prayer, remembering that expression is necessary to growth of maturity and understanding.)

1. Lord, I'm willing for You to make me willing. (To see Your way. To bear my inner cross. To do Your will.)
2. Lord, forgive me for insisting that others conform in outward things, thus making me their judge.
3. Lord, give me Your "accepting love" for others, especially for . . . (use first names only).

19

Maturity: a State of Being, Not Arriving

AN OLD GREEK MYTH ABOUT people who tried to solve their problems goes like this. Once a year a pilgrimage was made to the top of a beautiful mountain. Each pilgrim carried a scroll upon which was written a problem in his life from which he wanted to be free. Arriving at the top, he placed his problem-scroll in a beautifully carved chest, and he was then entitled to take out a scroll that someone else had deposited. He could exchange even that scroll if he was not satisfied with the "new problem" he had drawn out, but he had to take one with him when he left the mountain top. The end of the story? Each pilgrim finally departed with his own scroll, feeling that, after all, he preferred his own problem to any of the others.

Whether we choose the creative way out of our suffering, or whether we choose to become neurotic (refusing to face reality), this ability to choose is the dividing line between maturity and immaturity.

Reading a recent review on a book for teen-agers, I was impressed by the wisdom of the author. I was glad that the truth was plainly stated. The heroine, searching for answers to life, finally arrived at the end of her quest: she found out that no one had the answers. No "answers" exist.

But no one quite believes this. We all search for answers. We search for wise friends or counselors who can give us an answer, or at least some clue to an answer.

We reason that every problem has an answer if we can only find it. Food is an answer to hunger. Water is an answer to thirst. Hunger and thirst are signs of health, and our desires for these must be satisfied or health is impaired. Likewise man in his spiritual nature longs for complete rest and total release because God made him that way in order to help us find His answer. God does have an answer, but it is not usually in our terms of thinking.

His answer is in Himself, in fellowship with Him. He gives us His heart, His understanding, His thinking, His caring, His love. When we have Him, we are able to accept everything as from His hand.

This morning as I was preparing to write this article, I asked my friend, Anna Price, "What is maturity?" Her reply came out of her heart. "Accepting life as it comes, even though it is painful, and giving thanks to God — although I usually find myself resisting at first, and saying, Why does this happen to me?"

So often life doesn't turn out as we had expected. We pray about our plans, we feel "guided," we go ahead joyfully, and then suddenly God lowers the boom. What happened? What could have been done differently? If only, if only we had seen, or thought, or waited, or been aware.

"Not Without Tears" was the arresting title of a recent article. Didn't God make tears too? And they have their proper and improper use. Great release can be experienced through tears, or extreme selfishness can riot through them and choke all signs of maturity.

Whatever strikes home within you, as you read, I hope you will underline the passage. Then in your time of need, the subconscious mind has a way of presenting the truth to you in a fresh way.

I need to say the things I am writing, to myself as well as to you. For maturity is not a state of freedom from problems into which I'll someday arrive, but a state of being: an attitude of elasticity, an integration of hopes and contrasts, an acceptance of myself as I am, and a growing awareness of others.

None of these things is possible as long as we stay in our feathered nest, comfortably separated from the rest of the world, selfishly satisfied, refusing with hostility anything that might threaten to release us from the prison of our traditions. It is as if we must defend ourselves from any new thing which might bring growth or liberation (because of the hurt it involves).

Here we run straight into the problem of whether God is in what is happening or whether sin or evil is at the root. In either case, we may safely say: Christ can use what is happening to me, because He is a redemptive Saviour. I want to affirm that God uses problems and suffering to mature us. This He can lovingly do, because Jesus Christ learned obedience by suffering.

"After you have borne these sufferings a very little while," wrote Peter, "God will make you whole and secure and strong."

James tells us, "When all kinds of trials and temptations crowd into your lives, my brothers, don't resent them as intruders, but welcome them as friends! Realize they come to test your faith, and to produce in you the quality of endurance. But let the process go on until that endurance is fully developed, and you will find you have become men of mature character with the right sort of independence." James continues by stating that in case we don't know how to meet any particular problem, we only have to ask God, (without any doubts as to whether we really want God's help) and the necessary wisdom will be given to us. "Inward reservations reveal instability at every turn," he concludes at the end of his first chapter (James 1:2-8).

Paul insists dynamically that endurance produces wholeness or maturity. "As you live this new life . . . we pray that you will be strengthened from God's boundless resources, so that you will find yourselves able to pass through any experience and endure it with courage. You will even be able to thank God in the midst of pain and distress because you are privileged to share the lot of those living in the Light" (Colossians 1:11, 12).

The little plaque on the wall says "Prayer Changes Things." I wish someone would make one which says "Prayer Changes Me." To choose to give thanks to God, and do it from the heart, transforms endurance into acceptance with joy.

Maturity is a wholeness as opposed to an illness. Immaturity is an emotional illness. At a recent convention of medical men reported by the Chicago *Tribune,* this statement was made: "Eighty per cent of all the persons who seek help in a doctor's office are ill because of emotional disturbances."

A young woman who recently asked for personal counsel was unconsciously making herself physically ill because she was insisting that someone else act a certain way, so she would know how to act in return. To put any person in this impossible situation is to make them take the place of God in your life. Only Christ can tell us personally how we should be, and the way we should be. We cannot take our cues from people, but from the One who loved us unto death. "Father, forgive them" was His attitude.

Marriage helps some people recognize their need for maturity in personal relationships. After the honeymoon is over, responsibility descends and human nature reacts. What will happen then? Paul Tournier in *The Meaning of Persons* writes: "Marriage really means: helping one another to reach the full status of being persons, responsible and autonomous beings *who do not run away from life*" (*The Meaning of Persons,* Tournier, [Harper, 1957], p. 146).

Most of us, married or single, are always looking for protection; building little shelters against the storms of life, taking refuge in little safety zones from life's threatening traffic.

Being willing to meet the conditions of growth is a

decision only we can make. God is not in favor of our running away. He keeps us where we are, to work out our release and our emotional healing. By giving up our "rights to ourselves" and by refusing to place false guilt on others, we begin to cooperate with Him. We are aware of the impossibility of the situation, and we begin to see that our need is as great as the need of any other involved person or persons. This gives us love and tolerance and acceptance, both of them and of ourselves.

Let go of your beloved story, forget the odds against you. Let the other person off the hook (by ceasing your demands and criticisms) and put Jesus Christ on that hook.

Put your mind into forward gear, and never go into reverse again. Uneasiness will come because you are in new territory, but you can look into the face of Jesus Christ. He is always familiar and He is not upset by anything. Poise was the outstanding characteristic of Jesus' emotional life. All His emotions were intense but balanced, in full equilibrium. Peter says, "A calm and gentle spirit is a very precious thing in the eyes of the Lord."

"By an odd paradox, progress in knowledge of ourselves, is progress from uneasiness to uneasiness . . . a gradual feeling our way along a road of discovery, rather than a full and complete knowledge of ourselves. Integration is a progressive realization of one's secret propensities and a lucid and courageous acceptance of the totality of one's being, with all its complications and contradictions" (Tournier, *Ibid.*, pp. 83, 61).

Acceptance with resignation or rebellion is immaturity. Acceptance with joy is maturity. In *Pilgrim's Progress,* Christian found himself staggering under a burden he could not dislodge. Finally a Voice said to him, "Bear your burden quietly, and when it has served you, it will be taken from you at the Place of Deliverance without any effort of your own."

True maturity, or wholeness, comes through the welling up of Life, the Life of Christ within us. "Abide in me and I in you. Remain in me and I in you. Live in me and I in you." Life has its cycles of rest and activity, of winter and spring. When spring comes, and life is ready to burst forth, no one can hold it back. Life is not a state, it is a movement that results from perpetual incompleteness, which in turn can break into flowering branches of joy and love.

"When I was a child I talked as a child; I entertained child interests; I reasoned like a child; but on becoming a man I was through with childish ways. For now we see indistinctly in a mirror, but then face to face. Now we know partly, but then we shall understand as completely as we are understood. There remain, then, faith, hope, love, these three; but the greatest of these is love" (I Corinthians 13:11-13, *Berkeley*).

For Discussion

1. Read James 1:1-8 and Colossians 1:9-11, *Phillips*.
2. What do we learn from the Greek myth about the possibility of ending all our problems?
3. Do you know yourself well enough to face the real reason for your present search? Is this God's answer?
4. List some of the immature (futile) ways and attitudes mentioned in this chapter by which we attempt to escape from our problems.
5. List some of the positive marks of a maturing Christian.

Prayer Time

Silently

1. Leaf through the chapter, and list some of the practical things suggested that could help one who needs emotional healing.
2. Read the last four paragraphs again. Think through the implications of "accepting yourself with all your complications and contradictions."

Audibly (Depending on the number present, and the existing trust among them.) Invite individuals to pray for themselves. Jesus encouraged immediate asking and receiving, so ask, and others will help you claim the promise by giving thanks.

20

Decisions: Hearing God Speak to Us

Happy is the man listening to me, watching daily at my gates, keeping watch at my doorposts (Proverbs 8:34, *Berkeley*).

As A YOUNG CHRISTIAN, I was deeply intrigued by the subject: Hearing God speak. Does He really speak? Would He speak to me? Can I hear Him — hear a voice? Do I know it's really He? All on my own, as a teenager, I found the above verse in Proverbs, later I found Jesus Christ had a great deal to say about hearing in all of His teachings. Much later, other Christians taught me many practical aspects of listening to God.

Pictures suggest words, and words suggest pictures. As a child, I learned in grade school to look at a painting of one of the Old Masters, until I could make up a story. I remember a great dog, lying on a beach, with a child beside it. We were instructed to sit quietly and look at the picture, study it, think about it, put ourselves there and make up a story. It was fun.

In reverse, let the words in that opening verse at the beginning of this chapter, suggest a picture: First of all, there is a door, with gates, and doorposts. Then there is a servant waiting, watching. I expect he's sitting down, for most servants in the Near East sit rather than stand. Anyway, if he's waiting, he must be sitting. But he's not idly waiting, he's watching for something. He's watching for the moment those gates will open. He's waiting for the moment his Master will come and speak to him. He's listening for his Master's voice — as in the ancient Victrola trademark, a little fox terrier with his head cocked, sat there listening to his Master's voice coming from that big metal horn.

Then I mentally placed myself in that servant's place and thought of Christ as Master. This servant was probably purchased property; if not, then he was a love-slave, or a freed-slave. At any rate, he belonged to his Master, and since he was waiting at the Master's door, that must have been his special duty — to sit there and wait until there was an errand for him. Never mind what the errand, if the Master spoke, it was his pleasure to go, to move, to do as commanded, to obtain what was wanted. Maybe he had nothing else to do all day, except sit there at the door-posts, waiting. Sitting there quietly, his ears would become sensitive. First, he would hear the Master's footsteps, then he would hear the gate being unbolted, swung open, and there was the Master!

He would spring to his feet at the first sound of approaching footsteps. He would be respectful, attentive, ready to fulfill his calling as a good servant, for his Master loved him, and he found happiness in serving him. Out he would go on his errand, then back again, sitting quietly at the door-posts, waiting until his trained ears heard the Master's approach once more.

Happy, blessed, fortunate, to be envied is the man who hears the voicc of his Master, watching daily, waiting, keeping watch at his door-posts.

As the years passed, I began to recognize the quiet teaching coming to me from far down in my inner being — but from what source? That must be the Holy Spirit, the Teacher and Guide whom Christ promised would come to those who believed on Him. At once I knew that I could not literally waste time by sitting at some figurative door-post, waiting for a Voice that seldom is audible. I say seldom, because many Bible characters and some people since then have heard an audible voice, and I respect their receptive ability.

There is a time to sit quietly in meditation, devotion and prayer; there is also a time to keep one's ear open even in the midst of all the noises of our busy working world, right in the midst of the wishful clamoring of our devious hearts. It is the attitude that counts. The tone of the heart opens the ear.

Thinking and praying about writing this chapter has brought back so many experiences through which the Lord Jesus has spoken to me, guided me, led me, that I think I'd like to write a book on hearing God's voice.

Speaking of this desire, Lois, a friend, told me of an important business transaction, in which she was so definitely led and in which God spoke so directly to her, that she shared it with a number of her friends. "I was surprised and shaken through and through," she told me, "when this older Christian woman, herself a teacher of others, said wistfully, 'I've never had an experience like that. God's love is not personal to me. I know He loves the world, but if He loves me, why doesn't He speak to me like He does to you?' She went on to say that she used her mind, her common sense, tried not to rationalize and always did the best she could. Before she was through speaking, she was weeping, so great was her hunger to have a talk with God that would be personal." I asked Lois if this woman was a "born-again" woman. "Oh, yes," came her answer, "she certainly is. But she's like so many I meet, they seem to be walking around in a vacuum, not content with anything. When it comes to this world's possessions — they have far more than I."

There's another problem people have in hearing God's Voice. Another friend wrote: "I've been praying that the Lord would teach me His ways. I want to know when I'm serving Him, and when I'm not. It's not the temptations that bother me so much as knowing the difference between Satan and God. If I knew for certain which was the Lord's way and which the devil's way, I would be able to do His will with ease and serenity. It's this not knowing where I need the most help."

I'd add another clause to those two above, which to me complicates things still further. God's voice — Satan's voice — what about my own voice? God represents the highest good, Satan the opposite; while my own voice could be anywhere in the twilight between. And is it Satan or I who often comes along with something that represents "good" in order to steer us away from the "best" which God has for us? It is in this way that Satan appears as "an angel of light," and offers us something less than God's very best, which in itself is not necessarily wrong.

When I start writing on these subjects, I could easily become all wired-up and confused. First of all, I let the Lord Jesus take care of the evil one. He has, in fact, done that on the cross. In His wonderful words (John 10) on the Good Shepherd, He outlines the intimate relationship between Himself and His sheep. I trust absolutely in His intentions toward me.

According to Christ, all the sheep have to do is to hear the Shepherd's call, recognize His voice, and follow where He leads. He states positively that His sheep do not respond to nor follow robbers, strangers or wolves, because they do not recognize strange voices.

All the work of the Shepherd is in regard to His sheep: He calls each one by name, He cares for their needs, sees to it they are not hungry or thirsty; He leads them in and out, He Himself is the Door; He brings them abundant life, and He even lays down His life for them.

Like a stupid sheep, we often follow one another — into all kinds of by-paths where our Master has never been. Then we get caught, lost, or hurt, and hear His voice calling to us. At once He is there and we are safe again.

Life daily presents opportunities to follow the Good Shepherd. Our responsibilities concern others, and involve many decisions and choices which call for wisdom and discernment. We know we want His guidance in the big decisions of life, but in the smaller ones, we seem to muddle along making our own decisions. Then in sudden crisis with great distress and urgency, we call out for immediate aid, immediate directions. And there seems to be silence. No voice, no directions, no guidance. Silence? What's wrong? If God is there, and He loves me, and I'm His child, doesn't He know I need Him, and need Him desperately right now? He's there, but I don't know how to listen.

I had been a Christian about ten years before I met a group of missionaries in North China at the Pei-tai-ho summer resort who spoke of "hearing God's voice." I was immediately interested, hungry to hear more. I could think of nothing else. I wanted to hear Him speaking to me, guiding me. True, He had already led me in many things, and I had given myself to Him. I could already tell many experiences of His guidance.

Maybe it's the way the phrase is stated: *hearing God's voice*, that draws our attention. We know when things "work out" rightly for us that God has been at work, that He is planning and preparing for us. But to know ahead of time that He has spoken, that we are in His will, doing what He wants, without trial and error — isn't this what we all want?

More than that, I wanted to hear others tell their personal experiences in hearing God speak to them. What did He say to them? What did they do? How did they know? Were they always sure? These questions I wanted answered. But I only knew of this group by hear-say, I didn't know any of them personally, so how could I attend their meetings without an invitation?

Was it so strange that I met someone who invited me shortly after that? If I had known how to listen, I might have heard, "Daughter, leave it in My hands; I'll bring someone to you who will give you an invitation." And I could have waited with quiet praise, both before and after. But I didn't know how to listen that closely. All I could listen for was related to the big things: like giving my heart to Christ, giving my whole life to God, going to China as a missionary.

Attending an informal garden meeting, I soon found there was a price to pay — there usually is — to get my ears wide open. The price was honesty, open, clear, above-board honesty. For if one is not honest, so they said, there was always fear of the truth, and any attempt at self-protection would make me deaf, and not only unable, but unwilling to hear what God might be saying to me. At first I resisted this approach as being very unevangelical and unsound, but step by step God brought me to a place of honesty and true openness in my life, but that is another story.

My ears were opened. I learned how to listen, yet sometimes I still have trouble recognizing my Shepherd's Voice. "God is speaking all the time, all the time, all the time," I've quoted Dr. Laubach as saying this in a previous chapter. It bears repeating: "God is speaking all the time, all the time, all the time."

This very morning when I awoke, and had those first precious moments with Him, I suddenly remembered that today I had to write the chapter on, "Hearing God's Voice." And there are only three more days before I must leave for a week of meetings in Oklahoma. I felt myself become tense with anxious thought and fear. What exactly would I write? How should I select what is important from so large a subject? How could I make it plain to those who were ready to learn?

Suddenly, I smiled to myself and to my Lord. I would sit at His feet a little while. I would wait for His instructions, for they would surely come. He knows what is needed for this chapter. And it worked out like that. I trusted Him in that moment for the rest of the day, for the work of the day.

His word of comfort, advice, guidance, help, comes to me when I need it, not before. I can't turn right at the corner of Clark and Dickens, until I come to the corner *at* Clark and Dickens. Just so, I must go on, talking to Him in my heart, sharing everything with Him, knowing that when the time comes the directions will be there. Now let's put the same experience into these words: God spoke to me this morning. I felt myself becoming tense and anxious with fear. What would I write? I didn't know what to include and what to leave out.

Then I heard His voice in my heart and smiled as He spoke to me: "My child, I'm here with you. I'm with you always. I've helped you with every other chapter, haven't I? Just sit quietly with Me and wait for My instructions."

My anxious heart quieted down. I followed the instructions given. While eating my breakfast, I suddenly knew what was to be included in this chapter.

The other day a woman called with a question on hearing God speak. She said, "How do I *know* when I have God's guidance and when I've heard Him speak? Not long ago, I was sure He'd spoken to me, and when I did what He told me, it didn't work out." Questioning her a little, I found that she'd told the other party emphatically that God had sent her to do thus-and-so, and the other party couldn't see that God was in it at all. What was wrong?

My own experience has taught me to keep God's counsel reverently in my heart — before I tell someone else. Keep it, and think about it, compare it with what I know to be true of His character, and hold it there with an obedient attentive heart ready to move. If the door of circumstances opens, I move, quietly with sensitive steps, and follow the directions God seems to have given to me. Two things can happen: the door can close in my face, and I'll know I have the directions wrong. Or the door can open wide, and I'll know I got the directions right. In either case, I'll learn a great deal. In the latter instance, I'll be ready to share what happened with the person God chooses (His choice, not necessarily mine). It is often the wisest thing to hold our sharing until God has backed up our action. After all, a true testimony is a simple recounting of what the Lord Himself is like, how He has led, what He has done for us in a given set of circumstances.

The entire matter of hearing God's voice can be greatly simplified if we remember that the Kingdom is within. And the King is in His Kingdom. The Spirit of the Lord dwells *within.* Within the real me, within the real you dwells the Presence of God. "Not I, but Christ lives in me," wrote Paul (Galatians 2:20), recognizing this inner Presence in his own being. We never have to go out looking for Him; He's never away from us, always near to us. God is never preoccupied. He is always attentive and aware.

If you are responding to Jesus Christ, you are a Christian. You are a fulfilled, creative Christian if your response includes the *fact* that *His is an indwelling Presence* — our Lord with us and in us in every large and small happening in our daily lives.

For Discussion

1. Read John 10:1-15, 25-30. From this brief reading, find what the sheep do, what the shepherd does.
2. Discuss reasons given in this chapter, and from group experiences, discuss why people find it difficult to get God's guidance. (Include: pride, approval of others, fear of failure, perfectionism, etc.)
3. Discuss the relative importance of:
   a. Hearing God's voice and not obeying perfectly.
   b. Loving God and not hearing directions perfectly.

Prayer Time

Silently

1. Ask the group to sit quietly, with eyes closed for concentration, while a narrator (contact him the previous week so he may practice reading with quietness and pauses) reads aloud: the first six paragraphs of this chapter, including the Scripture verse.
2. Give the group time, now, to be quiet and think and pray without interruption.

Audibly

1. Repeat Psalm 23 in unison.
2. Invite someone to give a closing prayer.